SOVIET PRESCHOOL EDUCATION, Volume I:
Program of Instruction

SOVIET PRESCHOOL EDUCATION, Volume I:
Program of Instruction

EDUCATIONAL TESTING SERVICE
Henry Chauncey, Chief Editor

Holt, Rinehart and Winston, Inc.

NEW YORK   CHICAGO   SAN FRANCISCO   ATLANTA   DALLAS
MONTREAL   TORONTO   LONDON   SYDNEY

Foreword

In May of 1965 I visited the Soviet Union for the second time under the auspices of the U.S.-U.S.S.R. Cultural Exchange Agreement. The main purpose of the visit was to look at the methods of admission to the universities, the nature of examinations and the flow of students through the educational system. There was opportunity, however, to visit other educational institutions; and it was in the city of Urkutsk, deep in Siberia, that I was able to observe one of the kindergartens about which I had heard such favorable comment.

It was housed in a rather ordinary wooden building which contained a large number of cheerful, well-lighted rooms. If the building was not impressive, the equipment was: at the children's disposal were all sorts of games and toys, instructional materials, and athletic equipment. Each item had its particular purpose which was explained in a pamphlet available to the teacher. There were in all some 200 pamphlets on every kind of topic from how to teach children to dress themselves to how to have them tell stories in their own words. The over-all guide, of course, is *The Program of Instruction in the Kindergarten,* approved by the Ministry of Education of the Russian Republic and presented in translation in this book. *A Teacher's Commentary,* embodying much of the psychological and pedagogical theory underlying the program, will appear in Volume II to follow.

Because of the great interest in this country in early childhood education and because of widespread curiosity about how youth in the Soviet Union are being brought up, it seemed desirable to make the details of this program available to a wide American audience. The value of reading this volume lies partly in understanding the Soviet dedication to early training and partly in discovering the nature of what the Soviets consider an effective preschool and kindergarten program. The Russians pride themselves on giving children top priority. They speak of this frequently, and it is clear from the nature of the program and the careful thought that has gone into it that no effort has been spared to provide exactly the kind of environment and educational opportunity that they deem to be most appropriate, both for the development of the child and for the future of a communist society.

For all that has been written on American education, and for all the concern that Americans have *about* education, there is simply no parallel document of the Russian sort on our scene. Perhaps this merely reflects centralization of educational control in the Soviet Union as against our highly decentralized system. It may also reflect a lack of consensus on our part to produce a document that truly represents the present state of our knowledge and values about early education. It is quite possible that the intellectual and social predispositions that the Soviets desire to inculcate must be inculcated early, that the critical period for acquisition is long past when a child has reached the age of four or five. What the Soviets are doing is interesting and stimulating to consider, but we are a long way from knowing when formal education should begin and what we would consider a suitable program.

This translation should prove stimulating reading to those engaged in American preschool, nursery, and kindergarten instruction. In addition, since the early chapters of the book treat the first three years of the child's life, there will be points of interest to teachers in day-care centers and to American parents who are called upon to cope with their children during these formative years with the best care and intelligence they can muster.

These observations are by way of introducing the superlative Introduction that Professor Urie Bronfenbrenner has written for this volume. Professor Bronfenbrenner is uniquely qualified to speak on this subject, being at the same time a specialist on the Soviet Union and a specialist in early childhood education. He has visited the U.S.S.R. for extended periods of time on several occasions and is as knowledgeable as anyone in this country on Soviet educational policy and practice.

We are also indebted to Neale W. Austin and Mrs. Eugenie Vickery for the careful translation of the "program."

Henry Chauncey
Educational Testing Service

Princeton, New Jersey
March 1969

Introduction

This volume contains the operating instructions for the most extensive program of group upbringing in human history. Over 10 percent of all Soviet children under 2 years of age are currently enrolled in public nurseries. The corresponding percentage for children between 3 and 6 who attend preschool is about 20 percent. The enrollment is limited chiefly by the number of places available, with the demand far exceeding the supply. In Moscow, for example, which probably has more facilities than any other Soviet city, only 50 percent of all applicants can be accepted.

In the U.S.S.R. the use of communal facilities for the rearing of children is as old as the Soviet Union itself, but the program was considerably expanded in scope a decade ago with the creation of a new type of preschool institution, the *yasli-sad,* or *creche*-kindergarten, which provided for the upbringing of children from the age of two months to seven years (at which point the child is enrolled in regular school). The same Party resolution which established the *yasli-sad* commissioned the development of a new and detailed curriculum to be followed in all preschool institutions in the U.S.S.R. Responsibility for preparation of the new program was delegated jointly to the Academy of Pedagogical Sciences and the Academy of Medical Sciences. The present manual represents the outcome of that joint effort. It was first published in 1962. A second edition, with minor revisions and additions, appeared in 1965, and it is the latter version that is presented here in translation.

Although the manual was published by the Ministry of Education of the Russian Republic, it is in effect operative throughout all of the republics of the U.S.S.R. The Academy of Medical Sciences is an all-Union Academy; the Academy of Pedagogical Sciences recently became so. The writer has seen the procedures advocated in this volume employed, with only minor variations, in preschool centers ranging from Tallin, Estonia to Alma Ata in Soviet Asia. The present manual is used as the basic text for the training of all preschool personnel. In addition, it serves as the prototype for dozens of other works on preschool education published in the Soviet Union and in the socialist countries generally. This means that millions of children throughout the Communist world are being brought up in accordance with the principles and procedures presented in the pages which follow.

But the significance of programs of this kind goes beyond the Communist world. Given the nature of the changes taking place in all large industrial societies, including our own, there is every reason to expect that programs of group upbringing will become increasingly common in the Western world as well. In the United States, we have already seen the beginnings of the new trend in the rapid development of Project Head Start, which in the first two years of its existence has had 2 million children in attendance. Even higher enrollment figures can be expected if the Administration carries out the provisions of the 1967 Social Security Act. This calls for the establishment of a nationwide network of day-care centers to provide for the children of mothers who, according to the new legislation, cannot qualify for welfare payments (regardless of how young their children may be) unless they take a job or receive job training. Nor is the development of preschool facilities likely to be limited to disadvantaged families. The growing number of working mothers, the increasing importance accorded to a mother having "a life of her own," the ever-greater difficulties encountered in taking the child along for shopping or social visits, the unavailability of qualified household help; all these considerations—coupled with the experts' stress on the need for enriched cognitive experience in the early years—increase the demand for preschool programs among middle class families as well. With such major developments in prospect, we do well to examine the Soviet program if only to become aware of the problems involved, and how our own solutions might differ.

Although, as will become apparent, the manual leaves little to the imagination in spelling out what is to be said and done from hour to hour in a Soviet nursery, the Western reader may feel mystified or even be misled as he seeks to understand how the program actually works, primarily because he lacks the frame of reference which the Soviet authors, and their readers, take for granted. It is the aim of this introduction to convey some of this context. To begin with, the very title of the manual—and its central theme—presents problems of communication. The manual describes a program of *vospitanie,* a household word in Russian, but with no equally familiar English equivalent. The dictionary translates it as "upbringing," but perhaps more of the flavor is conveyed by the expression *character education,* for *vospitanie* is the process of forming the character of the young. In the Soviet context, it has an even more specific meaning—the development of what is called *communist morality.*

It is this moral emphasis which gives Soviet education its distinctive cast, at least in comparison with public education in the West. Moreover, it is this same moral emphasis which distinguishes the present manual from its predecessors in the 1950s, which focused primarily on subject matter rather than conduct. This point is emphasized in the *Teacher's Commentary* on the *Program of Upbringing,* which has also been made available in translation as a companion piece to this volume.

> In the *Kindergarten Teacher's Manual* (published in 1953), practically all of the mental and esthetic instruction was based on formal study. Such an approach led to a situation in which extracurricular instruction was exceedingly poor and limited, with the children being for all intents and purposes left to their own devices in the periods between regularly scheduled activities. Experienced teachers knew how to direct and enrich the extracurricular activity of the children in accordance with the educational objectives, but for the majority of beginning teachers this proved to be an extremely difficult and vague area, inasmuch as the "manual" was very obscure on this matter. The intensive and at times exclusive attention of administrators, teachers, and curriculum and methods study groups to problems of instruction (in the narrow sense) was typical of this period, when preschool personnel were absorbing the principles of kindergarten instruction, and it did yield positive results. But one must still be careful never to underestimate the education of children through so-called everyday life and to place this process in an equal position with that of more formal instruction. [p. 2]

The frequent references in the manual to the virtues of respect for elders, obedience, self-discipline, proper conduct, modesty, manners, and the like represent the initial statement of themes that are to be presented again and again throughout the child's educational career in preschool, school, and youth organizations. This brings us to the second distinctive quality of Soviet preschool education: its carefully designed continuity with the experiences to follow in school and in the closely associated communist youth organizations; namely, the Octobrists (grades I through III; ages 7–9), the Pioneers (grades IV through VIII; ages 10–15), and the Komsomol, or Young Communist League, which enrolls youth up to the age of 28 and sometimes longer. This continuity is especially apparent in Chapter VII of the manual, which is virtually interchangeable with the first chapter of analogous handbooks on upbringing for the primary grades, prepared by the same Academy of Pedagogical Sciences.

A third distinctive feature is hardly apparent in the text, but captures the attention of the Western observer the moment he enters a Soviet nursery. The playpens which he will see there differ in two respects from their Western counterparts. First, instead of being at floor level, the pen is raised on legs so as to permit face-to-face interaction between infant and staff memeber. In fact, the pens are at different heights depending on the stage of the child's development—higher for the supine babies than for the crawlers who begin to pull themselves up by the bars. But even more striking to the Western eye is the fact that each playpen is the size of a small room, and contains not one but half a dozen infants. Soviet children must learn to live in a collective society, and they begin to do so in the first year of life.

Nor is the development of collective consciousness left to chance. As toys, dolls, and other objects are presented to the children, the upbringer makes a point of explaining their communal nature: "Children, here is our dolly. Vanya, you give our dolly to Katya, Katya, pass it to Marusya; now Marusya and Petya swing our dolly together." The banner hung over the archway proclaims: *"Moe eto nashe; nashe moe"* ("Mine is ours; ours is mine"). Group play is emphasized, and children are discouraged from playing alone. I recall an incident in a Kiev nursery. As I watched, two upbringers suddenly scurried toward a corner of the room. "Aha," I thought, "there's a scrap and two kids have to be separated." But I was wrong. The Soviet equivalent of an emergency was one child playing quietly by himself. Not just interaction but cooperation is emphasized. Children are taught to work together, to help each other, and to be responsible for disciplining each other. The effect of this training is reflected in two contrasting observations, one made by me in a Soviet nursery, the other by a Soviet colleague visiting an American preschool center. I was watching the 3-year-old group at lunch. Just imagine 20 preschoolers at mealtime—one child doesn't want to eat, another calls the teacher, still another takes something from a neighbor's plate while the victim shouts his protest, someone else sings a song—laughter, crying, noise! Nothing of the sort. What I heard was the hum of subdued, civilized conversation. But it was not sound so much as sight that distinguished the Soviet scene most sharply from its Western equivalent. In any American nursery school, there would have been an adult sitting at each table. Not so in Yasli No. 239. Here the upbringers had already made progress toward the goal of "forging a self-reliant collective." The children were themselves responsible for keeping order.

The members of the collective not only discipline each other, but work together. This point was brought home to me by the comments of a distinguished Soviet psychologist, an expert on development during the preschool years. He had been observing in an American day-care center for children of working mothers. The center was conducted under university auspices and reflected modern outlooks and methods in early childhood education. It was therefore with some concern that I noted how upset my colleague was on his return. "I wouldn't have believed it," he said, "if I hadn't seen it with my own eyes. There were four children sitting at a table, just as in our nurseries. But each one was doing something different. What's more, I watched them for a whole ten minutes, and not once did any child help another one. They didn't even talk to each other. Each one was busy in his own activity. You really are a nation of individualists!"

Complementing the emphasis on collectivism is a stress on self-reliance. From the very beginning children are taught to do things for themselves. The notion is that by learning how to be self-sufficient, the child not only furthers his own development but also shows his consideration for others. I saw 18-month-old children dressing themselves (except for buttoning). In the third year they are already helping and taking turns at chores, such as setting table, cleaning up, or gardening. The development of a proper attitude toward work is regarded as a major aim of Soviet upbringing. As soon as the child learns to talk, this objective is pursued actively through games involving the role playing of various tasks, trades, and occupations (for example, taking care of baby, playing farmer, miner, steel worker). Visits are made to local shops and factories so that children can see workers engaged at their jobs.

Another distinctive approach for acquainting the child with the world of people older than himself is the institution of *shevstvo*. Literally, the word means "being a chief over," or "having under one's supervision," but *shevstvo* is actually best described as a system of "group adoption" in which a collective in the neighborhood, such as a third-grade class, a shop in a factory, or a section of an office or institute, takes the nursery group as its ward. Members of the collective visit the center, become acquainted with the children, make toys for them, take them on outings, and invite them to their own place of work. By serving as aids and models for the young, these older children and adults fulfill their general social obligation to participate in "bringing up a generation that will live and work under communism."

But if the rest of the community is more in evidence in a Soviet nursery school than in its American counterpart, there is one group that is less influential: namely, parents. The fact that they are scarcely mentioned in the manual reflects the extent to which the Soviet nursery is viewed as the domain of the professional educator, who "knows what is best for the child." In the Soviet system of child rearing, the role of the family is clearly subordinate to that of communal institutions, who carry the primary responsibility for upbringing. This message comes through clearly in the only extended reference to the family which appears in the manual:

> Every kindergarten should serve as a model of the Communist education of children. The pedagogical staff of the kindergarten is faced with the task of disseminating pedagogical knowledge among parents, helping families to bring their children up properly, and sharing their invaluable experience in family upbringing. And, as is indicated in the Program of our Party, 'the educational influence of the family on children to a greater and greater extent becomes totally integrated with their public education.' [p. 6]

This, then, is the context—ideological and social—in which Soviet preschool education operates, and in which the instructions of the manual are to be carried out. As he examines the detailed specifications it contains, the reader may ask how closely reality lives up to the recommendations. Do Soviet upbringers actually do what the book says? In response one may ask the analogous question for the American scene: does the American mother actually do what Spock or Ginott recommends? The answer is the same for both societies: she tries. If anything, the Soviet upbringer tries harder. For one reason, it is her full-time career; for another, she is not bombarded with contradictory advice from a dozen experts who disagree. There are many Soviet guidebooks on upbringing; but they all emphasize the same objectives and the same methods for attaining the goals. It is comparatively simple. But there is a problem: the products may also be the same.

But before the Western reader dismisses the Soviet approach as too steryotyped for his taste, he would do well to ask about our own efforts in this sphere. Whatever else one may think about Soviet methods of education, it is clear that the Russians have worked hard to develop ways for teaching their children, early in life, the values and *behaviors* consistent with Communist ideals. Are we doing as well for American society? What values and behaviors do we teach in our preschool programs? Or, to put it more provocatively, what values and behaviors do our children learn when they participate in these programs?

The answers to these questions may not be altogether disappointing, but even so, they prompt us to ask what one might find in an American equivalent to the Soviet manual, if such a book existed. There may be those who would argue that such a book should not exist—not a single manual for all programs. Agreed, but let us then have more than one. And, in the meantime, until they are written, we can read this manual and, on every page, ask with profit: how would we do it differently?

Urie Bronfenbrenner
Cornell University

Ithaca, New York
March 1969

Contents

VI

VII

SOVIET PRESCHOOL EDUCATION, Volume I:
Program of Instruction

Preface
to the
Russian Edition

The historical 22nd Congress of the Communist Party of the Soviet Union emphasized the immense significance of the Communist education of all workers and especially of the generation which is growing up in the period in which the building of communism will be proceeding on all fronts.

The leading role in the attainment of the objective belongs to public education.

With the purpose of improving the education of children of preschool age, the Central Committee of the Communist Party of the Soviet Union and the Council of Ministers of the Soviet Union on May 21, 1959 adopted a resolution entitled "Concerning Measures for the Further Development of the Institutions for Preschool Children and the Improvement of the Education and Medical Services for Children of Preschool Age."

This resolution called for the creation of combined preschool institutions for the education of children from two months to seven years old, and commissioned the Academy of Pedagogical Sciences of the Russian Republic and the Academy of Medical Sciences of the Soviet Union to work out a program for them.

A program of education for children up to seven years old has for the first time been worked out. This program defines the sphere of knowledge, skills and habits which are within the competence of children at various age levels to assimilate, and in addition describes the kinds of personal qualities which should be engendered.

With the new program, in contrast to previously published "Manuals," the requirements of the program have been kept separate from the methodological commentary.

The program of education differs substantially also in its structure. The objectives of the program have been designed to be realized in the course of all children's activity—in play, in regular activity periods, in the routine of daily life, and in forms of work within the capability of the children.

The oldest group in the program has been termed the school preparatory group. The content of the educational work in this group must comprise a reliable basis for successful study in school.

The program of education was developed by a joint commission of the Academy of Pedagogical Sciences of the Russian Republic and the Academy of Medical Sciences of the Soviet Union.

In the appendices to *The Program of Education in the Kindergarten* model daily schedules for the different age groups are provided.

A methodological commentary is being issued simultaneously with the program.

Introduction to the Text

THE OBJECTIVE OF THE KINDERGARTEN

The [Soviet] kindergarten is an educational institution providing for the public education of children from the age of 2 months until their entrance into school.

In the kindergarten the children are brought up in a society of their peers, which creates favorable conditions not only for personal contact with one another, joint games and activities, and the fostering of friendship and mutual assistance, but also for the development of individuality.

Public preschool education includes the physical, mental, moral, work and esthetic training and education of the children, and takes into account their age and individual differences.

Objectives of the Physical Education of Children

The [main objectives are the] care and strengthening of the children's health and their physical development. In the kindergarten the children must grow up healthy, cheerful, and spirited, well-coordinated, with good posture, loving life.

For the attainment of these objectives one must create a hygienic environment in the kindergarten, maintain proper and watchful care of

1

the children, follow the daily routine, and strengthen the child's organism.

Education of the Mind

In the kindergarten, a great deal of attention must be devoted to the development of senses, perceptions, speech, and thought.

Direct contact with adults is of decisive importance in the formation of the child's speech.

Children must learn to speak through the best models of their native language, and therefore it is imperative that the teacher's speech be correct in every respect.

One aspect of mental development consists in the familiarization of children with their environment.

The teachers must instill respect for working people, arouse interest in work, society, and nature. It is important to convey correct notions of the phenomena of inanimate nature and of plants and animals, to arouse curiosity and encourage an active relation to nature.

Moral Traits and Personal Qualities

Moral and personal traits should be developed in the children in the course of their stay in the kindergarten: the ability to distinguish good from bad, to do what one should and refrain from doing what is not permitted, to respect elders, to relate to children of their own age goodnaturedly, to help anyone in need, to be friendly in work and play, and to be truthful and modest.

In the course of play and activities it is essential to develop in the children qualities of well-being, self-control, and persistence.

Bringing the child up to love his native district and to respect and love the founder of the Soviet Government, Vladimir Ilich Lenin, is of great significance in his moral development.

Esthetic Education

The esthetic education of the children involves instilling in them a love for the beauty in surrounding life, in nature, and in art; developing in them an ear for music and poetry and the desire and ability to draw, model, sing, dance, listen to music, read poetry with expression, and tell stories.

Art renders the child more responsive and kinder, enriches his spiritual world, and contributes to the development of his imagination and sensitivity.

An attractive and comfortable environment, a clean building, and the neat appearance of children and adults help to develop artistic sensitivity.

Over the first 7 years of life the child covers a long road of physical and psychological development. The capabilities of the child are intensively developed, his moral qualities and character traits are formed, knowledge is accumulated and skills are acquired.

From the kindergarten, children will go on to school. It is essential to develop in the child those qualities which will enable him to learn successfully and with interest. The kindergarten children must be physically well developed; must learn to distinguish between play, activities and work; must be able to listen to the teacher and to each other, to perform assigned work at the necessary rate, and to act both in obedience to the teacher and independently.

All the elements of the educational work in the preparatory group—familiarization with the environment, mastery of the native language, computational skills, elementary grammar, musical training, and work habits—combine to establish a reliable basis for study in school. School should come to represent for the children that happy future which will give them so much that is interesting. The kindergarten establishes communication with the school which a majority of the children in the preparatory group will enter.

The many years of experience of the kindergartens and nurseries has made it possible to work out a program describing the basic content of the children's education (by age groups) from 2 months up to 7 years.

The educational program is realized in the daily routine processes, in play, in activities, and in elementary forms of work training, i.e., in every conceivable activity of children which helps to raise them to a new level of play, activity, and work.

The material in the program is arranged by quarters. The first quarter (September, October and November) coincides with the beginning of the academic year; the second quarter comprises December, January and February; the third March, April and May; and the fourth June, July and August.

FORMATIVE-EDUCATIONAL WORK IN RELATION TO THE ORGANIZATION OF THE DAILY ROUTINE

In a kindergarten where the children stay for the entire day, the daily routine, which includes eating, sleeping, conditioning, exercises and rest, must be organized in a rational way. These processes are repeated from one day to the next and create in the children a sense of a customary sequence of activities. It is important to develop in the course of these processes fixed habits of social behavior and continually to strive to make these habits more secure, so that when it is time for the children's transition to school, they will have already attained the necessary degree of refinement.

FORMATIVE-EDUCATIONAL WORK IN RELATION TO PLAY

In the preschool years play is of great significance for the physical and psychological development of the child, the formation of his individuality, and the formation of the children's collective.

As time goes on and the children's ability to imitate and their independence increases, the play of the children becomes more varied. Play enters into the life of the child, influences his development, satisfies his interests and makes possible the solution of various pedagogical problems. In their play children enter into definite relationships with each other, which gradually leads them into joint activities; their play evokes sensations of one sort or another. This enables one to make play one aspect of the organization of the children's life and of their interrelationships.

Play represents an important means of developing organization, collectivism, and the capacity for quick and precise action of one kind or another.

In proportion to their age the play of the children becomes more diverse in its content, form, and organization.

Games involving motion, educational games, musical games and role-playing games, all systematized in a definite way, are utilized by the teacher as a means of influencing the physical, mental, and esthetic development of the children.

FORMATIVE-EDUCATIONAL WORK IN RELATION TO ACTIVITIES

The realization of the program of formative-educational work is very closely related to the development in the children of the capacity for organized mental activity and the development of their desire and ability to study.

These abilities are developed primarily through the process of instruction in activities, although the vital prerequisites are acquired in daily work assignments and play.

Activities for infants actually consist in the personal contact of the adult with each individual child. This individual contact is very systematic in nature and is directed at the verbal and motor development of the children, their familiarization with the objects of everyday life and their functions, and with the work of adults.

With the development of voluntary attention and the capacity of the child to comprehend the words of an adult and to coordinate his actions with the actions of the other children, activities involving several children simultaneously, and then the entire group, become possible.

The instruction of the children is achieved through the activities. The modes and methods of instruction vary. They depend on the age of the children and the subject matter of the particular material in the program.

FORMATIVE-EDUCATIONAL WORK IN RELATION TO WORK TRAINING

Work training consists in getting children accustomed to the type of work which is within their capacity to perform and in engendering in them an emotionally positive attitude to the work surrounding adults.

The work activities of children in their preschool years have their origin in play, in the process of performing simple actions and tasks set by adults. They include various forms of self-service, routine housework, gardening and outside work, and the work involved in making one's toys. It is important to develop in the children a desire to do something not only for themselves, but also for others.

The kindergarten teacher's role is a highly respected and responsible one—to her falls the task of working out practical solutions to the problems in the public preschool education of children, an area given prominent significance in the Program of our party adopted by the Twenty-second Congress of the Communist Party of the Soviet Union; in this way the kindergarten teacher will actively participate in the building of communism in our country.

The education of the future citizens of a Communist society requires from the teachers in preschool institutions the gradual perfecting of pedagogical knowledge, study of Marxist-Leninist theory and the new program of the Communist party of the Soviet Union, participation in the political life of the country, and observance of the principles of the moral code of the builders of communism.

Every kindergarten should serve as a model of the Communist education of children. The pedagogical staff of the kindergarten is faced with the task of disseminating pedagogical knowledge among parents, helping families to bring their children up properly, and sharing their invaluable experiences in family upbringing. And, as is indicated in the program of our party, "The educational influence of the family on children should to a greater and greater extent become totally integrated with their public education."

I

The First Infant Group

FIRST YEAR OF THE CHILD'S LIFE

OBJECTIVES IN CARE AND INSTRUCTION

The preservation and strengthening of the health of the babies and concern for the correct physical development and conditioning of their organisms represent the most important tasks and goals of the teacher for this particular group. At the same time, the instructress must pay attention to the psychological development of the children. It is absolutely necessary to establish for the child a definite daily schedule corresponding to his age and physical condition and to develop in him a positive attitude toward washing, dressing, feeding, and going to sleep. It is also necessary to assure the proper rate of development of the baby's visual, aural, and tactile perception; his basic motor skills, hand movements, primitive manipulation of objects, vocal reactions, and aural comprehension. Toward the end of the year the baby should produce his first conscious words. The teacher must assure that the baby is happy and that he develops a positive attitude toward surrounding adults and children.

CHARACTERISTICS OF CHILDREN DURING THE FIRST YEAR

The first year of life is characterized by the most rapid rate of development. By 5 months the baby's weight doubles, and by 1 year it has increased to three times his weight at birth. Over the first year the height of the baby increases by approximately 25 centimeters. His body proportions also change significantly. By 7 months the weight of the cerebrum doubles. The efficiency of the central nervous system increases, and in conjunction with this the length of the waking periods also increases. From the first weeks of the baby's life, all his sense organs are developing; sight and hearing are of special significance for the general development of the child, since they enable him to form various contacts with the environment. Motor skills, manipulatory ability, and aural comprehension develop and the baby utters his first conscious words. Relationships with adults and children are established, and the baby's state becomes a happy one.

THE DAILY SCHEDULE AND THE ORGANIZATION OF THE CHILD'S LIFE

For children in their first year of life it is especially important to establish a correct daily schedule, since their physical development and emotional state depend to a considerable degree on whether they are fed at the proper time and whether they have slept well. The daily schedule should provide the baby over a 24-hour period with an amount of sleep corresponding to his age and physical condition, should specify a definite duration for each waking period and each period of sleep, and should establish the proper order in the alternation of waking periods, feedings, and sleep: after sleep, feeding; after feeding, a waking period; and then sleep again until the next feeding. With such a schedule one avoids the occurence of hunger pangs, one of the most frequent causes of a child's crying. When he has awakened the child is fed immediately, and when he is full, his waking period will be cheerful and active. A different sequence is permissible for children who are over 9–10 months old—they are capable of remaining awake and content for a while before feeding.

Within this group several different schedules should operate, since over the course of the first year the efficiency in the functioning of the cortex changes, and in conjunction with this the total duration of waking time over a 24-hour period and the length of each waking period increase. In addition, the number of feedings is decreased in the course of the first year, while the length of the intervals between them is increased. In establishing the daily schedule for children in their first year, it is essential that the following facts (see accompanying table) be used as a point of departure.

	UP TO 2½–3 MONTHS	FROM 2½–3 TO 5–6 MONTHS	FROM 5–6 TO 9–10 MONTHS	FROM 9–10 MONTHS TO 1 YR.
Number of feedings	7	6	5	5–4
Length of intervals between feedings	3 hrs.	3½ hrs.	4 hrs.	3½–4½ hrs.
Length of each waking period	1–1½ hrs.	1½–2 hrs.	2–2½ hrs.	2½–3½ hrs.
Number of times child sleeps during daytime	4	4–3	3	2
Length of each period of daytime sleep	2–1½ hrs.	2–1½ hrs.	2–1½ hrs.	2–2½ hrs.
Amount of sleep during 24-hour period	18–16½ hrs.	16½–16 hrs.	16–15 hrs.	15–14½ hrs.

The schedule should be set up to encompass the entire 24-hour period and should be observed not only in the kindergarten but also at home. In determining the daily schedule for each baby, it is important to take into consideration both his physical condition and his particular individual characteristics.

Physically strong babies who have a good appetite, sleep soundly for long periods and do not doze during the waking periods may be moved ahead to the next schedule somewhat sooner; weaker children require more frequent feedings and shortened waking periods, and as a result it is often necessary to keep them for a while on the schedule established for a subgroup of younger babies. It is extremely important to systematically check whether the schedule corresponds to the condition and capabilities of the baby, and to make changes in the schedule in case it does not correspond.

If the amount of food which a baby is receiving appears insufficient, and if when he is put to bed the baby does not sleep for a long time and then regularly oversleeps the feeding time, this may be an indication that he should be moved ahead to the schedule for the next age subgroup. However, one should not move a baby ahead to the schedule with only two daytime sleeping periods before he is 9–10 months old, since only at that age is he capable of remaining awake and active for a period of three and one-half hours at a time.

Arranging several different schedules according to which the waking period of one subgroup partially or fully coincides with the sleeping period of another will prevent the children from becoming exhausted and will give the personnel an opportunity to feed the babies leisurely by subgroups, care for them properly, and pay more attention to each individual baby.

To insure that the babies actually live according to the schedule, the following procedures are imperative: at the specific times designated for sleep, put the babies to bed in the open air and arrange conditions in such a way as to induce the babies to fall rapidly into a deep sleep; at the hours designated for waking periods, create conditions amenable to cheerful play and movement in the cradle or on the floor.

Sleep

For each period of daytime sleep (except on very hot days), all healthy babies in the infant group must be taken out into the fresh air where they fall asleep quickly and sleep well. At this time they spend five to six hours on the average in the fresh air. On dry autumn days, on sunny winter days which are not too cold, and especially in the springtime (March, April), it is best for the health of the babies to have them sleep in the garden or on open sun patios; on inclement days and when it is extremely cold, they should sleep on verandas. If there are no verandas, then the windows should be open in the room in which the babies sleep. One should never put babies to sleep in a room in which another subgroup of babies is awake and active at the time.

Children in their first year of life who have just entered the kindergarten and who, while at home, spent time outside become accustomed to the fresh air gradually.

One must develop in the babies the ability to fall asleep quickly and peacefully without the need of supplementary influences. Inasmuch as the whole process takes 20 to 40 minutes, it is possible, keeping within the allotted time, to put each baby to sleep at the very moment when he has played himself out and conceives a desire for sleep. The younger and weaker babies, and also those who woke up first the last time, must be put to sleep first; the older and stronger and those who woke up last are put to sleep slightly later. One must be very careful and thorough in dressing the babies for sleep in the open air, and in putting them to bed they should be prepared for sleep with soft soothing conversation. In putting the baby to bed, he must not be rocked, petted, or sung lullabies;

if the baby was accustomed to such actions at home, one should gradually break him of the habit.

Feeding

If a proper schedule is being observed, the babies will wake up gradually. As each baby awakes he is immediately taken up and fed. A baby who is sleeping should be awakened only when his mother has come for him, or after all those who have awakened have been fed.

Up to the age of 9–10 months babies are fed at home in the morning immediately after their nightly sleep, but from the time they reach 9–10 months of age they are fed at the kindergarten. During the day the mothers should come to feed their babies at the times designated in the schedule, or else they should leave off bottled milk at the kindergarten. It is important for the health of the baby that he have a good appetite, that he eat without fuss the entire quantity of food which he is offered, and that by the end of the feeding he is satisfied. In order to achieve this one must always feed the baby at the specified times, without haste develop in him a positive attitude toward food, and gradually develop his motor skills so that his activity while feeding will increase.

If a baby receives food from a bottle, then by the time he reaches 5 months of age he should be stretching out his hands to it, grasping it, and holding it during the entire feeding. From 4–5 months on the baby should be trained to eat from a spoon. Babies 5–6 months of age must be given the ability to eat satisfactorily foods which vary not only in taste but also in consistency. When the baby attains the age of 7–8 months, he should develop the ability to eat bread while holding it in his hands, and to drink from a cup held by an adult. Babies at this age eat while sitting in the arms of an adult. After a baby has learned to sit up by himself (from 8 months on), he should be fed at a table. From 9 months on when the babies are already sitting with ease at the table, the instructress feeds two babies simultaneously. For babies 10–11 months old a small rectangular table and a special little chair with a footrest are desirable. By this age the baby should be showing considerably more independence—in approaching the table with the help of an adult, getting into the chair, eating bread or cookies by grasping them in his hand, drinking from a cup by himself, and eating both solid and liquid foods.

While feeding babies over 6 months old the nurse names the motions and actions which the child makes and the objects connected with eating, and thus strives to control the baby's behavior verbally. The baby's understanding of speech manifests itself when upon the corresponding word he opens his mouth, takes and bites the bread, holds the cup, and produces other analogous actions. Toward the end of their first year children should be encouraged to pronounce certain words related to the process of eating.

While the baby is feeding, his face and hands should be clean, and there should not be any crumbs or drops on the table.

Beginning with the second half of the first year, when the baby is capable of holding bread in his hand, his hands should be washed before the meal.

The instructress and the nurse weigh each baby before and after he is fed by his mother; they carefully and without hurrying feed the babies whose mothers do not come, look after the sleeping babies, promptly lift out each baby who has awakened, and organize the play of all the babies who are awake. In order to maintain the schedule successfully, the instructress and the nurse should split up the duties—while one of them is feeding the babies, the other lifts out those who have just awakened and organizes play for those who have already eaten.

When the instructress approaches a cradle in order to put a baby in or to take one out to be washed, fed, or put to sleep, she should also pay attention to the other babies—speak to them affectionately and give them toys. This is vital in maintaining their activity.

Toilet

It is extremely important to train a child from the very first year of life to be neat. Thus it is essential to change the baby's clothes as soon as possible if he is wet or to wash him if he is dirty. One should develop in the child a positive attitude towards changing his clothes and utilize the process of changing his clothes for the development of motor skills, for increasing activity, and, from the age of 5–6 months on, for the development of an understanding of a few of the words which are associated with changing clothes. Toward the end of the first year the child stretches out his hands when he sees a brassiere, sits at the request of an adult, lies down, lifts up his leg and performs a few other actions.

Organization of the Waking Hours, Activities

Subgroup of Children up to 2½–3 Months Old From the first weeks of the baby's life it is important to develop his sight and hearing, since these are of great significance for the general development of the child and for his contact with the environment. One must also stimulate the baby to smile, hum, and move about. From the end of his first month of life, the baby can focus for an extended time on the face of an adult or on colorful or shining objects, and he can also follow them about with his eyes when they are moved; in the second or third months the baby's gaze is attracted by more diverse objects—he focuses on them more rapidly and for a longer period of time. From the first month on, one should develop in the baby the ability to listen to different sounds, to the speech of an adult, to the sounds of a rattle, a musical instrument, etc.

Special attention should be devoted to insuring that the baby develops positive emotional reactions in the proper time. The baby's first smile occurs in the third to fifth week while he is looking at the smiling face of an adult who is talking to him and while he is listening to his voice. In the second or third month the happiness of the baby manifests itself in more diverse ways—the baby not only smiles but also utters sounds, moves about energetically, rapidly straightening out and bending his arms and legs. These emotional reactions are useful to him since they increase his communication, strengthen his muscles, and aid in the development of vocal reactions and basic motor skills.

It is important to develop the baby's ability to lift and hold up his head while lying on his stomach and while in an erect position in the arms of an adult. In their first month babies, while lying on their stomachs, merely try to lift their heads. At two months they lift up their heads immediately, but do not hold them up for long. At three months they lie down with ease, leaning on their forearms. Putting a baby on his stomach is useful for the development of motor skills for strengthening the muscles, and for improving respiration and circulation.

From the very first months of life it is necessary to make an effort to prevent the acquisition of certain harmful habits—thumb sucking, drooling, falling asleep only while being rocked, etc. It is more difficult to break a child of bad habits than to prevent him from acquiring them.

From the time the babies are 1½–2 months old they are already spending their waking period in the nursery. There should be poles there for suspending toys. Strong, bright and sanitary toys should be suspended at a height of 50–70 centimeters above the baby's chest so that it will be comfortable for him to look at them. The babies should be dressed in swaddling clothes and warm shirts. Immediately after feeding, one may leave them wrapped up to their armpits in a blanket. Toward the end of the waking period one should unwrap the blanket so that the children can move about freely. The instructress should attend to the babies frequently, talk to them, attract their attention to toys, and make sure that they do not get cold.

In taking care of babies of this age, the following things are extremely important: (1) to develop visual-auditory concentration and the ability to locate with the eyes the source of a sound and to follow objects which are producing sound and are being moved along in front of the baby; (2) to evoke smiles, sounds, and typical lively movements by talking to the baby affectionately; (3) to develop in the baby the ability to lift and hold up his head while lying on his stomach by placing him on his stomach before feeding and before sleep; (4) to develop in the baby the ability to maintain a vertical position by taking him into one's arms from time to time and talking to him.

Subgroup of Children from 2½-3 to 5-6 Months Old   With babies of this age it is necessary to continue to develop sight and hearing and also the ability of the baby to fix his gaze on stationary objects and to follow moving objects not only while lying on his back, but even while on his stomach and while in a vertical position in the arms of an adult; to develop the baby's ability to recognize his mother, the instructress and the nurse; and to distinguish objects and sounds. By the age of 4 months the baby should learn to turn his head and to locate with his eyes the source of a sound—a noisy rattle or an adult who has hidden and is calling to him.

It is very important for the baby to be in a cheerful state throughout the waking period—to smile, utter sounds, and move about energetically. At about 4 months the babies begin to laugh aloud and they become attached to people who are affectionate toward them. At 3 or 4 months the babies make guttural sounds; at 5 months they add the vowels; and at 6 months they should already utter syllables (*ba*, *ma*, *pa*). It is important to encourage humming and babbling, since at this time the organs involved in articulation and aural attention are developing, and these activities will establish the necessary foundation for the development of speech.

Three and 4-month-old babies remain occupied for long periods with toys suspended above their chests. They repeatedly push against them with their hands, feel them, and grasp them. In the fifth month they try to reach a suspended rattle with their hands and to seize and hold it. By 6 months the baby begins to grasp it, not with two hands but with one, directing his hand with precision to the toy, no matter on what side it may happen to be. Having learned how to grasp toys, the baby occupies himself with them for longer and longer periods, looking at them, moving them from one hand to the other, and waving them about. Through these activities he becomes familiar with the properties of objects, improves his manual dexterity, and remains in a continually cheerful and active state. With the development of grasping movements, the baby develops a new need—to reach and take hold of a toy which has captured his attention. If it is at a distance from him or if it slips away, the baby may show real persistence, utilizing all the movements at his command and not infrequently devising new ones. The majority of babies try to crawl for the first time when they are attempting to reach a toy lying at some distance from them.

The proper rate of development of hand movements should be an object of special concern to the instructional staff.

It is imperative also to develop movements which are preparatory to crawling—by about 5 months the baby can lie for a long time while resting on the palms of his hands with his arms outstretched, and can turn over from his back onto his stomach. By 6 months he spends a good part of the time in a position on his stomach and begins to move about, shifting his arms. All these movements are of value in that they help to strengthen the muscles of the upper and lower extremities and to develop the baby's lungs and the muscles of the peritoneum. Moreover, these movements are indispensable in crawling.

One must pay close attention to the development of leg movements. By 5 months a baby stands securely when supported under the arms by an adult and by 6 months, when held only by both hands.

All healthy babies in this subgroup require more space to move around in than the babies who are not yet 3 months old, since by themselves they can now change position and move about. For the time which the babies spend in the nursery, they should be dressed (with the exception of hot days) in a little vest, a warm shirt, and swaddling clothes.

Toys for babies in this subgroup are suspended at arm's length above them. For 3- and 4-month-old children, one should suspend toys which will be easy for them to push against with their hands; for 4- and 5-month-old children toys which can be grasped only with more precise coordination of hand and arm movements. Starting with the age of 5 or 6 months, if the child grasps and holds objects well, he no longer needs suspended toys. The toys should be placed in front of him or put into his hands.

In all activities with children from the age of 2½–3 to 5–6 months, the following things are extremely important:

(1) to maintain a state of cheerfulness and to stimulate vocal responses to the speech of adults
(2) to develop sight and hearing, by showing the baby new toys and pronouncing the names of them—musical tops, wind-up toys, and others
(3) to develop hand movements
    (a) the ability to grasp an object from a position above the chest

    (b) the ability to grasp a toy located to one side of the baby or
        above his face, and to hold it for a while (from 4 or 5
        months on)
    (c) the ability to take a toy in each hand and hold both simulta-
        neously (from 5 or 5½ months on)
(4) to develop the movements preparatory to crawling
    (a) to put the baby on his stomach to enable him to raise the
        upper part of his body higher and to hold it up for a longer
        time
    (b) to stimulate him to turn over from his back onto his
        stomach (by 5 months)
    (c) to encourage him to crawl (from 5½–6 months)

In the plan of activities for each age subgroup it should be indicated
precisely which activities will be conducted and with which babies in
particular.

All of the indicated work is done in the form of separate activities with
each baby; moreover, these activities are not restricted to the time specially set aside for them but are also carried on generally while the staff
are looking after the babies. Only certain specific activities are conducted
with groups of five to six babies: the showing of wind-up and sound-
producing toys and musical activities.

The Subgroup of Children from 5–6 to 9–10 Months Old   In the care
and instruction of children of this age it is important to continue the development of the visual and auditory senses. Beginning with the second
half year of his life there is a sharp increase in the baby's interest in his
environment: adults, children, animals, toys, objects. The baby's reactions are more and more differential. He will come up to a familiar
person and try to communicate with him, while at the sight of a
"strange" person he may burst out crying. He follows the older children's
play attentively. He is persistent in trying to reach a toy which has attracted him. He listens to sounds and words pronounced by adults and
distinguishes the intonation of their voices.

Special attention must be given to the development of speech: the understanding of adult speech and the preparation for the control of active
speech.

The first manifestation of the baby's comprehension of speech occurs
in answer to a question about where a certain object, animal or person
is—the baby searches for it with his eyes and points to it with his hand.
In the beginning when an adult asks where something or other is and the
baby turns to the side where he is accustomed to seeing the specified
object, he is merely executing a movement which he has been conditioned

to make. But by 9 months he is already persistent in seeking out an object or person with his eyes, regardless of a change in its position. From the age of 6–9 months, babies also begin to distinguish the words and phrases used for certain actions—"Sit," "Lie down," "On your knees," "Wave goodbye," "Give me your hand"—and perform them readily.

The baby's understanding of the speech of those around him has great significance for his general development. A more complex type of contact between the baby and the adult is established. The baby is not only made happy by the adult's voice but also listens to his words and begins to comprehend a few of them.

If the baby knows the names of certain objects, it is easier for him to detach them from the over-all environment, and this capability is one of the indispensable conditions for the development of active speech.

The baby demonstrates his readiness for active speech by repeating various syllables over and over again for long periods at a time. He listens to the sounds of his own voice, repeats them again and begins to imitate an adult. From this point on, he utilizes sounds to attract attention to himself.

It is essential to create conditions which will further develop the baby's ability to manipulate toys. The 5- or 6-month-old baby treats all toys in approximately the same way—he examines them, moves them about, and bangs the toys against surrounding objects. By 8 or 9 months he is already distinguishing a few properties of the toys and is beginning to deal with different toys in different ways. For example, he will roll spherical toys, balls, and ovals. Smaller objects he will take out and put into larger ones, etc. Sometimes he strives to attain a specific result (he tries to put the smaller cup into the larger one, etc.). He occupies himself with toys for longer periods at a time.

It is extremely important to assure proper rate of development of various movements, particularly crawling. It is best for the baby to learn to crawl first, at 6 or 7 months, and then to learn to sit by 8 months. Having learned to crawl, he will go up to the very thing that interests him, get toys by himself, and move around a great deal. Crawling strengthens the muscles and helps develop coordination in movement. In order to use an object as a support, the baby must be able to crawl to it. Babies begin to crawl at 6 or 7 months. By 8 months they crawl rapidly for a considerable distance. Crawling on all fours is extremely instrumental in furthering the development of the body muscles and coordination of movement. In his eighth month the baby learns to sit up from a prone position and to lie down from a sitting position; to sit up without help; and also to stand up, take a step, and get down again while holding onto a rail with his hands. By 9 months he learns to walk while holding on with his hands to objects of various kinds.

Babies up to 7–8 months old can still spend their waking period in the nursery, but if their motor development is to proceed at the proper pace, it is essential that there be sufficient room there. Older babies who are already able to crawl and stand up with a support should spend their active period on a part of the floor which is partitioned off for them.

The instructress distributes the various toys in such a way as to stimulate the babies to crawl and so as to introduce a greater degree of complexity in their playing. One should never permit a baby to sit or stand for a long time at a stretch, since remaining in the same position for an extended period hinders the circulation of the blood and may lead to spinal deformation, pressure on the thorax, muscular lethargy, or general immobility. No less important is the prevention of the type of conflicts which may arise among babies if they gather in one place and get in each other's way.

The instructress utilizes every moment she spends with a baby for the development of his speech. In order for the baby to learn to isolate and comprehend specific words, the instructress talks to him in short sentences, emphasizing by her intonation the important word in the given sentences. She pauses after addressing the baby and waits for him to perform what he has been told. It is important for the word to coincide in time with the exact moment when the baby is doing the actions which have been named, is looking at an object which has been named, or is watching a motion or action being performed by the adult. In the speech of the nurse which is emotional and expressive, her loving, tender relationship to the baby should be reflected.

In activities with babies of this age the instructress develops an understanding of speech and enriches them with impressions. Toward this end she carries the baby up to various objects and shows him large bright squeaking and wind-up toys. From 8 to 9 months on she encourages the baby to pick out from a group containing many other toys the specific one named by the adult. For the purpose of familiarizing the baby with the names of adults and other babies, she leads a game of hide and seek.

In order for the baby to learn the words associated with certain actions ("Clap your hands," "Wave goodbye," "Give me your hand," "Reach as high as you can," and others), she teaches him these actions while accompanying them with the appropriate words. The instructress gets the baby to imitate sounds which he already knows how to pronounce, as well as new ones, to babble, and to imitate simple syllables. She develops motor skills (crawling, standing up, and walking with the help of a railing). She teaches him simple manipulations with objects ("Take out,"

"Put in," etc.). All activities should arouse the baby's interest and make him cheerful.

Work on the development of motor skills should be based on the activity of a baby, such as his efforts to approach a toy. For these activities it is better to use toys with which the baby has not previously played.

In order to give the babies satisfaction and to stimulate laughter and joyful exclamations, such games as "Hide and Seek" and "Billy Goat" are played.

The Subgroup of Children from 9–10 Months to 1 Year Old The most important objective in the care and instruction of babies of this age is speech development. The baby's understanding of adult speech increases significantly. He understands the names of surrounding objects, animals, movements and actions, as well as the names of adults and other babies. He willingly fulfills requests which he is able to understand. He will execute a definite movement or manipulation of an object. The words of the instructress will more and more frequently control the conduct and activity of the babies. She suggests to them what they might busy themselves with, how to use a toy, how to play together, etc.

By the end of the first year the babies are beginning to understand the meaning of the word "don't" (or "one may not"). Further development in the stage preparatory to active speech is evidenced when the baby repeats a variety of sounds and syllables over and over for long periods and repeats words spoken by adults. By the time he is one year old a baby can pronounce eight to ten words: *mama, papa, baba, dyadya, dai, idi, av-av,* and others.

It is extremely important to develop the interest of the babies in that which surrounds them: people, objects and animals. This broadens the baby's perspective, is satisfying to him, and represents an important condition for the mastery of speech.

It is important to instill in the baby a positive attitude toward adults and children. At this age the baby's need for communication with the adults around him increases. His interest in the things which others are doing is continually growing. Sometimes babies of this age play together. They throw little balls into the same basket, roll them one after the other down a slide, smile, and call to one another. If, however, the instructress is not sufficiently attentive toward the babies, negative relations between them may also arise, for example, out of an attempt by one to take a toy from the hands of another.

One must get the babies to perform more complicated manipulations with objects. At the age of 9 or 10 months to a year, the baby begins to perform certain actions directed toward achieving a specific result: taking objects out of something or putting them in, opening and closing toys with lids, taking rings off a post and putting them on, and putting little bricks one on top of the other.

Babies transfer their learning from one object to another. Thus, if one teaches a baby to open and close a box, then in a short while he will also begin to close a *matreshka*, put the lid on a saucepan, etc.

An important objective with babies of this age is to perfect the motor skills they have acquired and to develop the particular skills which will prepare them for independent walking. At 10–11 months babies are already able to walk while holding on only lightly to objects. They are able to move from one object to another and to go up and down stairs and inclines. By 12 months babies begin to walk by themselves without any support. This is extremely important for the basic development of the child. Once having learned to walk, he will be able to familiarize himself with an ever greater domain of objects and phenomena.

Babies in this age subgroup spend their waking period in a section of the floor which has been partitioned off by a railing and which is considerably more spacious than the nursery. Set out here is equipment of various kinds which will aid in the development of motor skills and the ability to manipulate objects: a ramp, a table with sliding drawers, etc. The babies are given pails, buckets, boxes with toys inside them, *matreshki*, little boxes and pans with lids, blocks of different sizes, colored rings, poles, a few "subject" toys, rubber dolls, etc. One should dress the babies in a shirt, vest, and overalls down to their ankles, socks, and light booties with leather undersoles.

In organizing the baby's play, the instructress demonstrates how to handle particular toys and watches to make sure that all the babies are happy and active. She helps create good relations between the babies and prevent negative types of infant behavior. She utilizes every moment with the babies for speech development.

In activities with babies 9–10 months to 1 year old, it is essential to continue developing the baby's active speech and his understanding of adult speech: to listen to the sounds and words they utter and to repeat them, to enlarge their familiarity with the environment, to help them discover new ways to handle objects, and to develop their ability to walk by themselves.

Activities with babies over 6 months old, as well as with those younger, must be carried on individually for the most part.

Following are activities designed to develop speech and to expand familiarity with the environment: showing animals (a cat, a dog, chickens, a bird in a cage); wind-up and squeaking toys; dramatizations with a doll; playing "The Magic Bag"; and showing pictures (from 10 or 11 months on). Games include "Show Me Your Ears" (the baby points to the appropriate part of his face or that of a doll) and "Find and Bring Me the Toy" (the instructress names the toy to be brought up). The instructress gradually complicates the games by, for example, picking toys of the same variety which differ only in external characteristics (rubber, celluloid, and rag dolls).

In activities aimed at developing the ability to manipulate objects, the instructress has the children put together toys which fit into each other (wooden pails, little buckets, balls, *matreshki*), take a ring off a post and put it on again, open and close a *matreshka*, put blocks on top of one another, etc. Performing these actions involves distinguishing properties of the objects—their size and shape—and requires definite persistence on the part of the baby. For example, in order to place the ring on the post, the baby will undoubtedly have to make several attempts. The babies pick out the objects necessary to complete the action (for example, if the baby is holding a toy saucepan, then he will look for the lid in order to close it).

In activities aimed at developing coordination, it is essential to stimulate the baby to move from one object to another; to roll down an incline; and, by the end of a year, to produce his first independent steps; to catch and roll a ball (while sitting); and to catch up with a ball, which is rolling. One should devise lively games for the babies: "I'm Going to Catch You," "Hide and Seek," etc.

Musical Training

Already in the first year of life it is extremely important to develop in the child an emotional response to music and the capacity to listen to music and be attentive to it. It is also essential to encourage the memorization of definite actions connected with the music (for example, the clapping of hands with the song entitled "Clapping Hands," hopping around to dances, etc.).

From the very first months of life the instructress hums the melodies of songs, while leaning over the baby's cradle and smiling to him.

Babies from 4 to 6 months old are gathered together in subgroups to listen to music (songs), and the music is accompanied by the showing of toys (a bright flag or tambourine decorated with ribbons).

In activities with the group of babies from 6 to 12 months old, the instructress, in addition to relaxing music, plays or sings dance melodies. She illustrates the songs by showing the babies "subject" toys with which they are familiar (for example, a dog, a bird, or a rocking-horse). The activities terminate in individual play or dance. The instructress encourages each baby to play or dance while she herself sings the song.

The instructress sings to the children or plays on a *mirliton* or *mitallophone* (toy instruments) such Russian folk songs as "The Little Hare" (without words), "The Cockerel," "Kotya-Kotok," "Bayu-bayu" (a lullaby) and the music of M. Krasev.

For the babies to accompany with various movements, the following Russian folk tunes are used: "At Our Gate," "I'll Save Up Gold," and "The Good Woman."

The following songs are performed and illustrated by the showing of toys: "The Little Bird" and "The March," music by M. Raukhverger, and "From Under the Oak Tree," a Russian folk tune.

II

The Second Infant Group

SECOND YEAR OF THE CHILD'S LIFE

OBJECTIVES IN CARE AND INSTRUCTION

The most important goal of the instructress is to continue to safeguard and strengthen the child's health, to condition his body, to promote emotional stability and an active and cheerful disposition, to initiate training in neatness and self-sufficiency, and to develop basic locomotor skills (walking, climbing, throwing, and running) and hand movements.

It is important to teach the child to use certain household objects and toys, to continue to develop his visual, auditory, and tactile senses, to develop in him elementary conceptions of objects and their properties, to develop his ability to imitate and improve his comprehension of the speech of those around him, and to develop the child's own speech; to teach him to observe the established rules of behavior, to maintain good relations with the other children and affection toward his mother and other adults.

CHARACTERISTICS OF CHILDREN DURING THE SECOND YEAR

With proper training, further physical and psychological development occurs in the child: the monthly increase in weight is from 200 to 250 grams; in height, 1 centimeter. The structure and functioning of the internal organs, the bones, the muscles, and the nervous system all improve. By 2 years of age the child has already 20 baby teeth. With the appearance of the molars (1 year and 6 months to 1 year and 8 months), food requiring chewing (unpolished vegetables and cutlets) should be introduced into the child's diet. The improving heat regulation of the body makes it possible under sanitary conditions to lower the water and air temperature. The efficiency of the nerve cells increases; the active waking period of the children from 1–1½ years lasts for three to four hours, while for children from 1½–2 years, from four to five-and-a-half hours. The amount of sleep in a 24-hour period decreases from 13½ to 12½ hours. The length of each period of daytime sleep for children from 1–1½ years is between two-and-a-half and one-and-a-half hours. Children from 1½–2 years sleep once during the day, for three to three-and-a-half hours.

Of vital significance for the development of the child are his relations with adults: he develops the ability to imitate, which is of great significance in the molding of his behavior and in particular in the mastery of speech and the development of play activity. The adult shows the child ways of using household objects and toys. Through imitation the child, after 1½ years, begins to reproduce in his play not only actions shown to him by adults but also that which he observes in surrounding life.

In children in their second year of life the visual, auditory, and tactile senses are being further developed, and elementary conceptions of surrounding objects and their properties are being formed. By 1½, the child fully recognizes familiar objects regardless of changes in color, size, or shape. By the end of their second year, children are capable of distinguishing words which sound similar, of recognizing and naming familiar melodies such as "Song of the Kitten" and "Song of the Puppy."

The child's understanding of the speech of those around him develops rapidly, and by the end of the second year he understands simple stories. The number of words which he can say increases (from 10 to 12 words at 1 year of age to 300 words at 2 years). Toward the end of the second year the child begins to speak in sentences involving various parts of speech. For the child, speech becomes the basic means of communication with adults, while the teacher's speech represents a means of regulating the child's behavior. The child talks a great deal while playing and while engaged in other activities.

The child walks confidently, overcoming natural obstacles such as ditches and mounds, does a lot of climbing, begins to run, to throw a ball, to roll a ball in a definite direction, to master simple dance movements, and to imitate the motions of adults and other children. His hand movements are developed.

The child's ties with those around him are strengthened: he communicates with adults on very diverse matters and learns rules of behavior—not to take toys away, to sit at a table calmly, to play without interfering with others, to obey the commands of an adult, and to do what he is told. Children still cannot play together for extended periods, but relationships between them are steadily growing and becoming even broader in nature; the children imitate each other in play and may help each other by lending one another toys, etc.

ORGANIZATION OF THE LIFE OF THE GROUP AND THE CARE AND INSTRUCTION OF THE CHILDREN

Children from 1 year to 1½ years sleep twice during the day for periods of between two-and-a-half and one-and-a-half hours; after they are 1½ years old they sleep only once, for three to three-and-one-half hours. Therefore, although the children together consititute one instructional group, they are living by two different schedules. Within each of these subgroups, the children who are younger are put to bed first and awakened last. If a child of 1 year 6 months or 1 year 7 months, who has been moved up to the schedule with a single period of daytime sleep, becomes sluggish or on the contrary over-excited, he should be put back for a while on the schedule calling for two daytime naps. Breakfast should be served no later than one hour after the children have been awakened, and dinner, for children over 1 year 6 months no later than four hours after breakfast so that their waking period does not exceed five to five-and-a-half hours.

Depending on how well the children master the necessary skills, it may be possible to feed and undress them simultaneously in groups of two, three or four; the adult washes or undresses a few children while the remaining ones are playing. After a meal or after dressing, children start playing again without waiting for the others. In the younger subgroup the children are fed dinner in the order in which they awake.

The teacher trains the children to do things by themselves and encourages and helps them in this self-reliance.

In the course of the first year and a half, it is important to teach the following skills: to eat bread and soup and, beginning with 1 year 2 months to 1 year 3 months, to use a spoon. By 1 year and 6 months the child should eat the food he has been given by himself; on a word from the teacher he should move his chair back after eating and get the necessary clothing; take his shoes and socks off, rinse his hands, and express his requests and desires by gestures, mimicry, and the words available to him.

In the latter half of the second year it is important to teach the children to wash their hands, to stay neat while eating, to use napkins, to pull up their socks and overalls while they are being dressed, to understand the significance of objects and to name them. The instructress familiarizes the children with the most characteristic qualities of objects used in eating, dressing, and washing (for example, "The jelly is sweet," "The water is warm," ". . . cold," etc.). Special attention should be devoted to training the children to obey the commands of an adult and to carry out the adult's requests. By the time he is 2 years old, the child should know his place at the table, should know where his towel and clothing are in the cupboard, and should be able to sit calmly at the table; he should have learned how to take off parts of his clothing which have already been loosened or unbuttoned by an adult.

During that part of the waking period not devoted to more formal activity, eating, getting ready for bed and such other processes, the instructress creates conditions in which the children can play with toys, building blocks, and natural materials, can move about freely, observe the surrounding environment, and look at pictures. The instructress should talk with the children and answer their questions about all sorts of things.

All children in this group sleep in the open air during the day (on a veranda with open windows) the year round.

In the winter the children in the older subgroup have two outdoor recreation periods every day, each one lasting for one hour: after breakfast and after their afternoon snack. In the summer the entire life of the children is transferred to a play area outdoors (sleeping, eating, instruction, and playing).

The schedule for children in their second year changes with seasonal conditions and the length of time the children spend in the kindergarten.

For the group which remains at the kindergarten for the entire 24-hour period, the schedule is set up in such a way that children in the younger and older subgroups are together for only a limited period of time (from 5:30 to 8:00 P.M.). This helps to prevent them from getting over tired.

With children in their second year, activities are conducted in the following areas: (1) the development of speech and orientation to the environment; (2) the development of locomotor skills; (3) ability to manipulate objects; (4) musical training.

These activities can be carried on individually or in groups: the activities aimed at developing speech and handling objects are carried on in groups of four to six children, while for musical training and active games, groups of ten to twelve children are formed.

Speech Development: Orientation to the Environment

In the second year, the period of intensive speech development, it is important not only to continue to develop the child's ability to comprehend the speech of those around him but also to develop the child's own speech, both in the routine of everyday life and in special activity periods.

First Half of the Second Year By the time he is 1½ years old, the child should know the names of the people around him and the names of many of the objects which are found in the kindergarten. He should obey the simple commands of an adult ("Get the toy," "Bring your shoes," etc.); should be able to point out the paws, tail, eyes and ears of toy animals; should know where his own hands, feet, and eyes are; where the buttons are on his shirt; where a pocket is or a bow; he should recognize familiar objects in real life and in pictures; and he should understand the basic themes of little dramatizations by the teacher with toys presented or the characters of a doll theater.

In developing active speech in children up to 1½ years old, it is essential to encourage imitation and to develop their ability to listen attentively to an adult's speech and to answer not by gestures but by the words available to them.

By the age of 1½ years, the child should imitate with ease words and combinations of sounds which he has heard frequently, should babble a great deal, and should accompany his activity with a rattle.

Latter Half of the Second Year To develop the child's comprehension of speech, one should call his attention, both during routine, everyday activities and during activity periods devoted to objects and pictures, to the qualities, the shape and the purpose of familiar objects; one should teach him to distinguish between objects which are similar in appearance and teach him to understand an adult's story about things and events connected with his own personal experience—even when the story is not accompanied by a demonstration involving objects, pictures, and actions.

By the time he is 2 years old, the child should have adjusted to his immediate environment; he should use the names of foods, dishes, furniture, clothing, and toys which he encounters frequently; should call adults and children by their names; and should know the names of animals; he should understand the main subject of a picture, get the gist of a conversation between adults in which they are speaking about events familiar to him and carry out the oral requests of an adult.

In developing the child's active speech, it is essential to encourage him to turn to adults as often as possible with all sorts of questions, to make sure that simplified versions of words in the child's speech are replaced by the correct forms, and to train the child to express his wishes and requests in words and short sentences.

When the aforementioned pedagogical objectives are stressed, the child will express his requests in simple sentences of two, three, and sometimes four words, each word in grammatical agreement with the others.

To develop the child's power of perception and his ability to conceptualize, one should periodically alter the setting in the common room and the play area (hang new pictures; change the toys; dress up the dolls in different clothes; put new plants, preferably flowering ones, on the windowsills and shelves; bring in for a time a bird in a cage; etc.). One should call the children's attention to these changes, arouse their interest in the activities of the adults (the assistant, the janitor, and others) and the activities of the older children, get them to observe animals and natural phenomena (for example, "The sun is shining," "It is raining," "It is snowing").

In all of this, one should observe along with the children and name the object and the action involved: "The carpenter is banging with a hammer," "The driver is starting the automobile," "The assistant is washing the dishes," "The bird is flying," etc. In certain cases one should name the qualities of objects and their functions, make simple comparisons for the children, and make generalizations (for example, "Today is a holiday," "Everybody put on a pretty dress," and "The children are waving flags").

The recommended number of activity periods per week aimed at speech development and orientation in the environment is: 24-hour groups—six to eight, day-student groups—four to five, including the conversations and observations during the outdoor recreation period.

Recommended Activities

(1) Showing objects and naming them—"The Magic Bag" (from 1½ years on)
(2) Games based on searching for objects
(3) Showing objects in action, "subject" demonstrations (from 1 year 4 months to 1 year 5 months)
(4) Showing animals (cats, dogs, birds), both in the street and in the room
(5) Special excursions—through the building, around the grounds in the summer (from 1 year 3 months to 1 year 4 months on) and off the premises (after 1 year 6 months to 1 year 8 months)
(6) Playing with pictures: showing pictures and naming the objects and actions (from 11 or 12 months on). The child selects a picture at a word from the adult: pictures with an illustration

on one side, blocks with pictures and paired pictures (from 1 year 3 months to 1 year 4 months)

(7) Reading, by the instructress, of poems, amusing stories, and jokes, in order to have the children chime in with little comments ("Yes" and "They all flew off," etc.)

(8) The game, "Listen and Show How a Cat Meows, a Dog Barks, or a Cow Moos," an exercise in articulation (from 1 year 3 months to 1 year 4 months)

(9) Repetition of familiar words, one after another

(10) The game "Perform the Errand" (bring a certain thing, put it over there, show how a ball bounces)

(11) Reciting short nursery rhymes

(12) Stories and conversations about things the child has seen often and knows very well (from 1 year 3 months on), and also about things which are going to happen in the future (from 1 year 6 months on)

Physical Development

The children develop physical skills in the course of the daily routine, through active games and through exercises. For the groups of children in their second year, there are three periods each week for exercises and two or three for active games (including the games played during the outdoor recreation period). The active games and exercises should keep the children happy.

One of the fundamental objectives in relation to children of this age is the improvement of their ability to walk under various types of conditions: to walk through grass, to get over mounds, to walk along limited surfaces (such as along a board), to step over obstacles (such as ditches), to step over a stick placed on the ground, to step to the side, to move backwards, and to turn around in place slowly.

It is essential to develop in children around the age of 1½ years the ability to climb up a little stepladder, to climb over a log, to climb under a bench, and to climb through a hoop.

One must teach the children to roll balls, throw them back and forth to each other, drop them, and throw them for distance and for accuracy.

The instructress develops the child's ability to move and dance by himself and to accompany songs and music with various sorts of movements. She also trains the children to perform together a few motions and actions.

Physical Development in Children Up to 1½ Years

Walking The child should be able to walk up and down a board, one end of which has been raised 10–20 centimeters above the ground (width 25 centimeters, length 1½–2 meters); to get up onto an overturned drawer, 10 centimeters in height, and then to get down again; to step over a rope or pole raised 5 to 10 centimeters above the ground.

Crawling [The child should be able] to climb up and down a small stepladder, bringing the feet together at each step or advancing with alternating feet.

Throwing [The child should be able] to throw small balls into a horizontal target, a basket with a diameter of 60 centimeters at a distance of 20–40 centimeters.

Physical Development in Children Up to 2 Years Old

Walking The child should be able to walk up and down along a board (width 25–20 centimeters) which has been raised 20–25 centimeters above the ground; to get up onto an overturned box which is 50 by 50 centimeters and 15 centimeters in height, and then to get down again; to step over a pole or rope which has been raised 12–18 centimeters above the floor.

Climbing [The child should be able] to climb up and down a stepladder, bring both feet together or alternating left and right feet forward.

Throwing [The child should be able] to throw a small ball at a horizontal target which is even with the child's chest and at a distance of 50–70 centimeters.

Suggested List of Active Games and Dance Games for Children from 1½–2 Years Old "Clapping Hands" (words and movements by N. Blumenfeld—folk time); "Aida" (words and movements by G. Il'ina); "The Bubble" (*Active Games for Preschool Children*, authors M. Kontorovich and L. Mikhailova); "Tay" (words and movements by J. Plakida); "The Big Ball and the Little Balls"—a large ball is rolled and the little balls are thrown around and gathered up; "The Goat Is Coming"; "The Children and the Dog" (words and movements by N. Blumenfeld); "Where Are You, Vova?"; "A Bear Took a Walk in the Woods" and "They Ran into a Cozy Corner" (words and movements by N. Pappe); "Let's Play Hide and Seek" (words and movements by N. Kruglyak).

Development of Dexterity with Objects: Towers, Put-Together Toys, Building Materials, etc. By the time they are 1½ years old, the children should be learning to reproduce actions through imitation: put three to five rings on a post, open and close a *matreshka* or jar without difficulty, put objects into them which are considerably smaller in size, drive wooden pegs into the slots in a little bench, place several building blocks one on top of the other, place them side by side, reproduce simple constructions which they have been shown by an adult (a tower or a fence), and put the blocks back into the box after playing with them. The children should know the names of the toys they are handling and the actions they are performing; and using the words available to them, they should be able to call the adult's attention to the results of their activity.

In activities with children from 1½–2 years old, one should utilize the children's ability to handle objects for the further development of manipulatory skill and visual perception; one should call the children's attention to the size of objects, to sharply constrasting shapes (spheres and cubes), and to basic colors, by naming these qualities at the appropriate moment.

By the time the children are 2 years old, they should be able to keep at an activity which they have learned until they have achieved a definite result: they should be able to lower all six to eight rings onto the post and assemble a tower out of rings of various sizes, which are now less sharply differentiated than previously. In activities and active games they should perform several sequences of actions, for example, take blocks out of the box; make a simple structure, previously demonstrated by the adult (a gate or a train); and then put the blocks back into the box again. Working by himself the child should be able to reproduce easily structures and perform various actions involving objects, when these have previously been demonstrated by adults. He should be able to distinguish the contrasting sizes of objects; name objects and actions; and, through words and sentences, call the attention of the adult to the results of his activity.

In order to develop the children's ability to manipulate objects, activities are carried on in which the children (1) assemble and tear down a tower; (2) lower beads onto a thin pole (by the end of the second year), put together and take apart a *matreshka*, and roll little balls around.

With children 1 year old, activities are organized with table sets of construction materials; from 1½ years on finer toys and sand are used.

Through the process of manipulating objects, new abilities begin to appear in the children. Their development is dependent on repetition and the help of an adult. With the children who are not yet 1½ years old and who are boarding at the kindergarten, activities are carried on four or five times a week; for day-children, three or four times. With children from 1½–2 years old, three to five activities are carried on every week.

In the individual activities for the children in their second year, manipulating objects should rank of no less importance than playing with "subject" toys.

PLAY

Children's games involving "subject" toys, educational toys, and construction materials are organized outside and inside the building.

Play with "Subject" Toys

Objectives   By the time the children are 1½ years old, it is important to have trained them to carry on purposeful activity with some sort of "subject" toy; to play with the toy in a particular way; to develop their ability to imitate a visual pattern, i.e., actions demonstrated by an adult; and to train them not to get in each other's way while playing.

By imitation, by direct prompts from an adult, or by his recollection at the sight of the toy (feeding a doll, winding it up, putting it to bed, etc.) the child should be able to reproduce in a game actions which are already familiar to him and which he observes anew; he should be able to play with toys in rather definite ways, to find the objects needed for continuing a game, to transfer actions which he has learned from an adult in connection with one toy to another analogous one.

With children between the ages of 1½ and 2 years, one must continue to work toward developing more stable behavior in their play with "subject" toys and to develop their conceptions of the qualities of objects used in games, the kinds of sounds produced by familiar animals, and their characteristic habits (for example, the way a cat walks, the way a bird chirps and hops about, etc.). This latter type of development is enhanced by introducing greater variety and complexity into the individual and group observations of the environment and into the teacher's demonstrations and dramatizations. The children are trained to follow certain simple rules in their play: not to get in each other's way, to share toys, to give another child a toy which he needs, and to participate in games involving a sharing of roles (one loads blocks onto a wagon and the other unloads the wagon).

By the time he is 2 years old, the child's play should be relatively stable and diverse. He should be reproducing in a game several related and sequential actions which previously were familiar to him only separately (feeding a doll, putting it to bed, and then taking it for a ride, etc.). He should be able to imitate, immediately or shortly after, various new actions which he has observed in his surroundings. One should teach the children while working with "subject" toys to use additional play material; to replace "real" objects, for example, a block instead of a piece of soap, a stick instead of a thermometer; the children are also urged to introduce themes into their active games.

In playing with educational toys and building materials, the children perfect skills which they have developed previously.

Musical Training

The objective of musical training is to develop the child's ability to listen attentively to the melody and the words of a song, to imitate the sounds, to repeat the words and syllables which are relatively simple in structure, and to perform dance movements which correspond to the content of the song.

By the end of the second year, children, during a lullaby, will say to their dolls "bayu-baju" [*go to sleep*].

At the age of 1½ years, children listen to the melodies of songs played on a *mirliton* or *metallophone.*

When the children are between 1½ and 2 years old, the instructress sings songs, accompanying them with the appropriate movements. (Sometimes, but not always, she will illustrate the song with appropriate toys.)

In drills involving objects (toys, flags) and in dances, the children at first perform movements as indicated by the instructress, and then (at the age of 1½–2 years) they perform the movements according to the words of the song. In dances they hop on one foot; march in place; with upraised or outstretched arms, turn their hands up and down; etc.

Children 1½ years and older enjoy "marching," i.e., walking around the room to music and, following the example of the teacher, trying to raise their feet up higher.

Musical activities are conducted two or three times a week with children between the ages of 1–1½ years and twice a week with children from 1½–2 years old.

Musical Works: "The Goat Is Coming" and "The Hare," Russian folk songs; "Mary-Mary," a refrain; "The Little Bird"; "The Puppy," music by M. Raukhverger; "The Cat," music by A. Alexandrov.

The songs listed above are accompanied by the showing of toys and movements.

For the children to accompany with movements, the following are used: the Russian folk songs "The Hare" and "Clapping Hands"; the Belorussian folk song "Yorochka"; the Ukranian folk song "The Leap"; and "Look What We Can Do," music by E. Tilicheeva.

In addition, music and songs should be heard outside of the regular activity periods.

III

The First
Younger Group

THIRD YEAR OF
THE CHILD'S LIFE

EDUCATIONAL OBJECTIVES

To protect the children's health, further develop and condition their
bodies, and promote stable active behavior and good emotional
adjustment

To broaden the child's orientation to his surroundings; to develop
his ideas and elementary conceptions of objects, qualities and
phenomena; to continue the development of speech and rational
thought

To improve coordination; to develop the play activities of the
children; to expand and strengthen good relationships among
the children and between the children and the adults; to train
the children in group behavior

To further develop simple habits and skill in doing things independently; to train the children in good health habits and manners;
and to get the children interested in performing simple chores

To instill in the children an interest in and a love for, music, singing,
poetry, and stories

CHARACTERISTICS OF CHILDREN DURING
THE THIRD YEAR

With proper instruction during the third year, fundamental changes
take place in the development and behavior of the child. Although at a

35

somewhat slower rate than during preceding years, the weight of the child steadily increases (on the average 2.8 kilograms over the year), as does his height (7–8 centimeters). The bone structure of the child hardens; the functional development of all his organs continues, although since they are not yet fully developed the child is still very vulnerable. The upper limit of efficiency of the nervous system is raised; the child can remain active for an uninterrupted period of 6 to 6½ hours, while the necessary amount of sleep over a 24-hour period decreases to 11½ to 12½ hours (2 to 2½ hours during the day); he can remain occupied at one activity from 15 to 25 minutes. The child develops the ability to control himself and restrain his desires and actions; but he is still incapable of lengthy anticipation, cannot remain in the same position for a long time, tires quickly, and becomes overexcited when the nature of his activity does not change sufficiently.

As a result of an improvement in his coordination, the child develops greater flexibility and dexterity and becomes more self-sufficient in eating, dressing, playing, and other activities.

The child's speech develops rapidly, which significantly alters his behavior. The content of his speech is enriched, and his vocabulary is enlarged. The child begins to use (although not always correctly) all parts of speech and to make long and complex sentences. By the time they are 3 years old, children pronounce all sounds with the exception of *r* correctly, although in certain combinations they occasionally mix up certain sounds with others. Speech becomes the basic means of communication, not only with adults but also with other children. The child begins to grasp the casual relationships in frequently recurring events and makes primitive comparisons, deductions, and generalizations.

In their play the children tend more on their own to imitate the actions of the people around them. Group games begin to develop. By the end of the third year, elementary forms of "role-playing" games are being played. It becomes possible to teach the children new activities: manipulating a pencil leads to attempts at drawing, playing with blocks gradually leads to construction. In the second half of the third year, a child, before performing an action, will frequently define in words what he is about to do: "I am going to draw an airplane." He will more and more frequently be guided in his actions by his previous experiences, which have been integrated into his ideas and conceptions.

The children take an active interest in what is going on around them. They carefully observe the work of adults, natural phenomena, and animals. Moreover, the children are not satisfied by simple observations of their environment but demand explanations and pose the questions: "Why?" "How come?" "Where?" "When?" They begin to compare objects and events, although their impressions are still superficial, fragmentary, and unstable.

The children love to look at pictures, and while doing so talk incessantly and ask a multitude of questions. They listen with interest and attention to what adults tell them.

In spite of considerably greater independence in their play, children left to themselves for a long period, even in their third year, cannot find something to do. As a result of this, they become sluggish or, on the contrary, overexcited.

Through his activities and his relations with adults, the child absorbs more and more knowledge and formulates more conceptions of his environment; his experience broadens. He becomes better oriented to the common room, to his own home, etc. On the basis of experience and under the influence of instruction and the assistance of adults, the child's ability to obey the elementary rules of conduct improves; his relationships with adults and other children become more complex.

Children help each other and show interest in the activities of their friends. The child's emotional experiences become more diverse, as do the reasons behind his emotional reactions. The child experiences many positive emotions in his reactions to the environment and in his personal contacts with adults relating to his achievements. His emotional response to music, singing, and literature becomes more and more pronounced.

ORGANIZATION OF THE LIFE OF THE GROUP AND EDUCATION OF THE CHILDREN

A single schedule is established for the group, but games and activities, outdoor recreation, and the process of going to bed are all carried out in subgroups.

The schedule set up is a 24-hour one. The children should receive their breakfast no later than one to one-and-a-half hours after they have awaked.

A child of 3 years, when compared to one of 2 years, eats considerably faster and wastes less time in washing, dressing, and other routine processes. As a result, more time may be devoted to play and activities.

Children 2 or 3 years old, even when dressed in warm clothing and footwear, can still walk along the street fairly easily and freely. The duration of a walk may thus be extended to one-and-a-half hours. In cold periods, the children have outdoor recreation twice a day. When warmer weather sets in, some of the activities are moved outside.

If the children are given a daily sponging at the kindergarten, they should be given a shower once a week at home, just before going to bed at night. If, however, they do not receive these spongings at the kindergarten, they should then be bathed twice a week. For healthy children, sponging is recommended year round.

During the summer months children are put to bed 30 to 40 minutes earlier than in the winter. Their daytime nap is proportionately lengthened. Play and all activities are organized on the playground. If on the playground there is a section which is protected from the sun, dust, and noise, then sleeping and eating are also organized outside. When the hot weather sets in, the children are sponged on the playground before dinner, and their feet and bodies are washed before they go to bed at night.

It is important to organize meals, sleep, outdoor recreation, and toilet routines in ways which will insure that the children have a good appetite, will fall asleep quickly and peacefully, and sleep for a sufficiently long period of time; it is also important to make sure that the children receive sanitary care. All of these things contribute to making the children's behavior active and their dispositions cheerful.

It is essential to make certain that the children maintain correct posture while eating.

In the third year, the routine processes of dressing, washing, and eating should be utilized to the greatest possible extent in the development of speech and physical coordination, in improving adjustment to the environment, and in molding stable behavior.

One should further develop previously acquired skills through frequent exercises, and develop greater self-sufficiency on the part of the child.

In his third year, the child should be trained in the following skills and habits: washing his hands before meals, eating neatly, and using his right hand predominantly; by the time he is 3 years old, the child should be holding his spoon correctly, using a napkin, and getting it before the meal and putting it back afterwards; he should not be getting up from the table until he has finished eating and should not be interfering with other children during meals; he should say thank you after the meal, wash and dry his hands by himself, put on and take off various items of clothing and footwear, unbutton and fasten the buttons in front, untie shoelaces, know the right order in undressing and dressing, and put away promptly clothing which he has taken off.

One must train the children to use only their own individual sanitary objects; their own individual handkerchiefs, towels, and chamber pots; to wipe their noses by themselves, to notice when their hands are dirty or when there is something wrong with their clothes (a sock has fallen down, a button is missing, etc.).

One should get the children interested in performing various chores, for example, helping the instructress take toys out to the playground and getting the materials for activities and putting them away. A child over 2½ years old can even assume simple responsibilities consisting of a series of related actions, such as helping the assistant place the chairs at the table before a meal or bringing in the bread plates. Taking care of oneself and performing chores represent the initial forms of work training.

The instructress should name the objects and actions with which the child comes in contact, explain them, and define the qualities and functions of the various objects.

Care of the children should be organized in such a way that they do not have to wait for each other. When he has finished washing his hands, the child begins to eat without waiting for the other children to sit down at the table. The children do not all dress at the same time and so not all have outdoor recreation together: part of the group starts to dress while the rest continue to play. The children who are dressed go out to the playground with the instructress, not waiting for the assistant to dress the remaining children. One should dress the children warmly but lightly, so that their clothing does not encumber their movements. The children should be outdoors as much as possible. On the playground, conditions are created which will enrich the children with a variety of impressions and which will permit a variety of games to be played.

On the playground it is essential to have little benches or couches on which the children can sit and rest.

In the summer it is important to have available the playground toys and equipment for various types of physical activity: monkey bars, gymnastic ladders, hoops, balls, etc.; natural materials (sand, water); and equipment for active games and table activities. In the winter the children need shovels, sleds for sliding down hills, sleighs for their dolls, etc.

The instructress provides for alternating the various types of activities and games during the outdoor recreation period.

In her everyday contact with the children, the instructress broadens their perspective. Their orientation to their environment promotes sensory development and the development of physical coordination and speech. She directs the attention of the children to what is going on around them and talks with them about a variety of things: for instance, about where a child went with his mother on the previous day, who gave him the little shovel, where so-and-so is, why she is no longer in the group, etc. She calls their attention to what is beautiful in nature and to the objects and sounds in their environment. The instructress should stimulate the desire of the children to speak. Whenever possible she transforms a word from the child into a conversation, gives verbal commands, and in every way possible encourages a child to relate to adults and to the other children. She develops in the children boldness and persistence, stimulates them to make a real effort to achieve a particular goal, and helps them to overcome difficulties which they are unable to cope with by themselves.

It is essential to instill in the children positive social feelings and to train them to observe simple rules of group behavior.

The child should readily obey the requests of the instructress—to go and eat, to wash one's hands, and not to disrupt order in the sleeping room; to talk quietly and to lie down peacefully without disturbing the others.

The child should say "hello" and "good-bye" and express his desires in words, calmly and without any yelling.

By her own example and her words, the instructress teaches the children to talk to each other affectionately; she encourages them to assist each other (undo a button, pass a bread plate to the child sitting adjacent) and to help the younger children.

The instructress should spend time with each child not only in order to develop and mold proper behavior but also to cheer them up by singing a song, reciting a rhyme or lullaby, or caressing them.

PLAY

Games play a very important role in the lives of 3-year-old children. Along with "subject" games, they play many games without a definite theme or subject: they roll balls and spin tops; they not only handle small toys but also sort them out according to color, size, and shape; in their play the children walk, run, and climb a great deal.

Children in their third year can play a particular game or remain occupied at a given activity for a period of 15–25 minutes without a break. The play of children is of greater duration and is more concentrated. Although individual games still play a significant role, the children already begin to play in groups of two or three, since they are now able to coordinate their actions with those of others to a certain degree.

Educational Objectives

To insure that the children have a cheerful disposition and are sufficiently active

To perfect their physical skills and their speech

To evoke joy and a feeling of satisfaction

To develop positive relationships among the children

To diversify their play and introduce greater complexity into their games

One must teach a child in his third year to say what and with whom he is going to play, how he will use a particular toy, etc.; one should make his conceptions more precise, develop his attention, his thought, and his memory; encourage frequent verbal communication with adults and with other children; and develop in the child the habit of taking care of toys and equipment.

Organization of Play

All free time should be given over to the children for active independent activity. Toward this end it is essential to make available to the children all sorts of toys and equipment.

During the outdoor recreation period and also when the children are inside the building, the instructress should call their attention to the actions of surrounding adults and older children and to the animal life; she herself should perform various things in the children's view—draw, build, repair toys, etc.; stage little dramatic scenes, tell stories, show illustrations, etc.

Children in their third year are already more independent in their play, but their games will nevertheless be repetitious and primitive if the instructress does not guide them. She should suggest new games and make the children recollect and reproduce certain actions which they have previously observed. By directed questions, she should get the children to make the games they have begun more complex; she should encourage and train the children to play together; and she herself should participate in the children's games.

While making a choice available to the children in their play, the instructress at the same time should bring about a diversity and an alternation in the children's play activity by providing additional toys or removing certain ones or simply by giving instructions: she switches children from one activity to another and alternates activities involving considerable motion with other more restful ones.

In the morning hours the instructress is busy receiving the children. In advance she should take away the complicated equipment (folding pictures, mosaics, etc.) and games which require her constant observation. Large pieces of apparatus should not be available at this time. In the morning when the children come into the common room, they play with toys with which they have already become very familiar, build with blocks, load dolls into wagons, look at pictures, etc.

In the interim between morning breakfast and the activity period, the instructress should not encourage games which are too similar in nature to the activity which is to follow.

Just before sleep one should draw the children into relaxed games of various types.

Supervision of the children's play must in no case tend to destroy their initiative: it consists in lively and enthusiastic contact with the children and taking into account their development, interests, and individual differences.

In order to maintain in the children a cheerful, joyful disposition and also in order to develop positive emotions, the instructress organizes "diversion games"—games of "Hide and Seek" and "Tag"—and also shows them amusing wind-up toys, "magic" lanterns, and slides. The children derive great satisfaction from familiar active games and dances and amusing dramatic presentations of puppet theaters. In these amusements, positive emotions are instilled. The words of the instructress and the actions involved should amuse the children and give them real pleasure.

Types of Games

"Subject" Games   In their "subject" games, the children begin to represent not only actions which they themselves have frequently observed (going to sleep, eating, dressing, etc.) but also activities of surrounding life which are more distant from them (such as, for example, the work of a driver, a barber, etc.). Many more details enter into their play; for example, the doll's hands are washed before she is fed, and when she is being fed a napkin is tucked in, etc.

Toward the end of the third year, the children devise role-playing games in which they perform definite roles. They not only feed and put the doll to bed but also portray the mother or doctor; they announce in advance which role they themselves intend to play: "I'll be the doctor" or "I'm the mother and this is my daughter." The roles are still not stable, and the children frequently change them. For the development of role-playing games, the participation of the older children is desirable.

Active Games   Children in their third year assimilate the content of a game much more rapidly than children who are not yet 2 years of age; they become more confident in their movements and less frequently require the direct help of an adult. In their games they are able to portray birds and hares.

Gradually, the themes and content of the games broaden, and the ground rules become more complicated. For example, with the help of an adult the children form a circle, perform a certain role at the command of the instructress, and then turn away while one of their classmates hides.

More complicated ways of combining actions are introduced into the games: dancing in pairs while holding hands, turning around and running in the opposite direction. Active games are repeated two or three times.

Following is a suggested list of active games: "Tag," "The Rooster," "Ball," and others.

In active games changes of pace are important—there should be a transition from relatively relaxed to more lively movement; movements requiring intense effort and those permitting relaxation must be alternated. One should never, however, require children of this age to make a rapid transition from one type of movement to another.

Educational Games   For children in their third year, it is important to have games which will encourage them to distinguish and name colors (red, blue, green, yellow); and shapes (sphere, cube, brick), which will lead to the formulation of elementary numerical concepts (many, a few, one, two), and which will develop the children's visual and auditory perception, delicate motor skills, the ability to imitate, and the power of attention.

These goals are achieved through the following educational games: toys which can be assembled and disassembled (*matreshki*), little buckets, balls, and towers with rings (of one color or of various colors); jigsaw puzzles with four to six parts (starting from the age of 2½ years); the games "Ku-Ka-re-Ku" (inventor V. Fedayevskaya), "Paired Pictures," "Large and Small," "Do What Has To Be Done," "Pictures with Rhymes" (author N. Aiges); and many other games in which the child is presented with the problem of comparing and selecting pictures according to a definite role (for example, for an animal, select its young), finding the objects mentioned in a particular rhyme, etc.

The following are games designed to further auditory development and orientation to the surroundings: "Let's Listen and Name What We Hear"; "Tell What Is Making the Noise" (a bell, a drum, a fife); "Try and Recognize Who Is Talking"; "What Am I Doing?"; "Do the Same Thing As I"; "Tell What Has Been Hidden"; "Guess What Is in the Bag."

As the children master the educational toys under the direction of the instructress, they begin to use them independently. The instructress watches to see that the educational toys are being applied in the way intended.

ACTIVITIES

In the third year, the independent activity of the child increases beyond that of the previous year; but the child still cannot keep busy by himself for a long period. Therefore, for each waking period there should be one activity and one organized game. In the cold seasons, one of these is carried on in the building and the other outside on the playground, while in summer all activity is transferred to the playground.

Activities in speech development, activities which involve new material and require the explanations and help of an adult (jigsaw puzzles, new construction sets, etc.), and physical exercises are conducted in small groups (six to ten children).

The group is not subdivided for musical activities or routine activities with building materials nor for puppet theater, film, or dramatic presentations.

In the second half of the third year, when the children have already mastered the essential manipulations and learned how to use a pencil properly and how to use clay, drawing and modeling are also conducted with all the children at one time.

Activities involving new material should be repeated more frequently so that children become more secure in the skills involved.

The duration of the different types of activities and games will vary between 7 and 20 minutes and will depend upon the particular type of activity and the children's stage of development. Storytelling and drawing should last from seven to ten minutes while musical activities, modeling and activities involving building materials may continue for 20 minutes.

For the various activities, the children selected for each subgroup should be more or less at the same stage of development.

Speech Development; Broadening Orientation to the Environment

Objectives

To insure further development in the child's comprehension of the speech of surrounding people, to enrich the child with visual images and impressions, to train him to understand oral speech without visual illustrations, and to enlarge his active vocabulary. ˙

To teach him to pronounce sounds and words correctly. To teach him to talk in sentences, to convey his impressions, and to answer questions.

To develop emotional expressions in his speech.

To develop further his ability to listen to short stories and poems.

To develop his ability to look at pictures by himself, to look at books, to talk about them, and to handle them properly

For speech development and orientation to the environment, the following activities are conducted: systematic observations (for example, "Look how the building is decorated for the holiday," "See how they are removing the snow from the playground," "Watch how the children ski"); special excursions (for example, to the older children's playground, to the woods to pick flowers, and others; educational games ("Look What We Have Here," "Name What You See," "What Does Each One Need?" "Lotto," and others [see special section]; dramatic presentations with simple themes and the use of toys as props (for example, "How the Disobedient Kitten Burned His Paw"; "How Natasha's Little Bird Almost Flew Away," etc.); working with pictures—looking at pictures representing separate objects and actions, simple themes; looking at several pictures connected by a common subject. For such activities one may use, for example, the books: *Toys* by A. Barto, *My Teddy Bear, Katya's in the Nursery* by Z. Alexandrova and others; showing of slides accompanied by a story told by the instructress; discussions concerning what the children saw on a walk, what toys the children have at home; discussions about a forthcoming holiday, about what they are going to do on a walk, etc; telling fairytales, reading stories, poems, anecdotes, for example: "The Speckled Rooster" (a folk tale), "The Cat and the Goat" by V. Zhukovski, "We Lived with Grandmother" (a folk tale), "The Baby Sparrows," "Lullaby," "The Toys" by I. Plakida, "The Ball," "The Rabbit" by A. Barto, "The Holiday" by A. Taitz, and the folk songs "Clapping Hands," "The Boy's Little Finger," "Kitten, Kitten"; stories by the instructress about what the children themselves have not directly seen but can understand on the basis of their own past experiences (for example, how a boy was sledding, fell down, and hurt his leg); games for developing the vocal cords, for example: "Tell Who Sounds Like This" (a crow cawing, a large dog barking, a puppy barking, etc.).

Utilizing the children's impressions of their environment, the diversity of their routine activities, and the special activity periods, the instructress should work to strengthen the children's conceptions of the phenomena of inanimate nature (the sun is shining, it is snowing, it is cold today); knowledge of the plant world (a flower, a tree, grass, a leaf, an apple, a carrot, a strawberry plant); knowledge of certain events in the life of society (today is a holiday, red flags are all about, there are many people in the street and the children are receiving presents); knowledge of the work of adults (the nurse is washing the dishes or is watering the flowers, the driver is steering the car, the doctor is taking care of the children, etc.); knowledge of everyday events and the purpose of household objects (one sleeps on the bed, one eats at the table, one pours milk into a cup, soup into a dish). One should develop elementary spatial concepts (near, far, here, there) and concepts of time (morning, evening, later, now, tomorrow, today).

Children should learn to understand simple relationships between events (it is raining, there are puddles in the street; the cup was dropped, it has broken).

With proper instruction, the child's speech reaches a significant level of development by the time he is 3 years old.

The child understands the gist of an adult's speech about things around him and things which are related to his experience. It becomes possible to talk with him about his past impressions, about what he is going to do, where he is going, etc.

The child repeats with ease everything which he hears, and he memorizes short poems and little songs. His vocabulary reaches 1200 to 1300 words and includes all parts of speech, with the exception of participles and gerunds. The child uses sentences with many words, and subordinate clauses begin to appear in his speech (although grammatically the sentences remain incorrect). He talks a great deal with adults and children about various things and can, when prompted by questions, relate the content of a fairytale or story which he has heard. His speech is emotional and expressive. His pronunciation is basically correct with the exception of the sounds *r*, *l*, and the sibilants.

Physical Development

Objectives

To encourage further development in walking, running, climbing, and throwing

To develop the ability to stop at a signal, to change from one type of movement to another, and to change speed

To assist in the elimination of superfluous motions, to mold more economical and rhythmic movements, to teach proper posture

The child develops physically in the routine of everday life, in games (especially active games), and through walks. In addition, in accordance with the instructions of the doctor, specific sets of exercises are performed each week.

By the time he is 3 years old, a child should be able to walk along a straight or inclined surface (along a board 15–20 centimeters in width, raised 25–30 centimeters above the floor); step over obstacles (for example, across a cross-bar at a height of 25–30 centimeters); go up and down a stepladder; climb up and down on wall-bars, 1½ meters in height, drawing his feet together at every step or alternating right and left feet forward; throw a ball at a vertical target which is at a level even with his eyes and at a distance of 100–125 centimeters; throw and catch a large ball at a distance of 70–100 centimeters; coordinate his movements with those of other children (for example, walking in pairs and walking around in a circle); use his hands and feet simultaneously (for example, stamping his feet while clapping hands); change in his speed, his direction, or the style of movements at a signal from the instructress (for example, shifting from a fast run to a walk); hold himself back (although still with difficulty) and wait for signals (for example, "Do not run until someone says one, two, three," "stand still and don't take the flag off the floor until the very last words").

Drawing, Modeling, and Activities with Building Materials

Objectives

To develop interest in drawing, modeling and construction; to teach the child to use a pencil properly (holding it in the fingers of his right hand, not too close to the point; drawing straight, curved, and zigzag lines, closing them to get circular and angular forms); to use clay (breaking off little pieces, wetting them, and rolling them); to use table sets of building materials and to make designs consisting of simple elements (poles, wheels, walls, and the roofs of houses)

To encourage the representative function of drawing, construction, and modeling and the repetition of the things the child has discovered how to make; to get the children to be able to copy the elementary structures which have been demonstrated to them; and to develop the child's ability to see what an adult or another child has represented in his drawing or construction

To teach the child to follow definite rules: to draw only on paper or on the blackboard and not to tap with his pencil, to use his materials neatly and not to smear the paper, to model at the table and not to throw the clay around, to clean up his material at the end of the activity period, and to sit properly at the table

While the children are drawing, modeling, or working with building materials, the instructress teaches them how to hold a pencil, shows them how to roll clay, and how to draw, for example, a road. She explains to them what one has to do to prevent a structure from falling down. Sometimes she herself draws, builds, or models various objects which are easy to copy (for example, she models a carrot or an apple, draws a fence or a ball, builds a house or a garage; then she has the children try to recognize what she has made).

If the activities are carried on regularly throughout the year, children 3 years old will be able to use pencils, clay, and building materials correctly.

They enjoy drawing, modeling, and building and name their own structures and drawings according to any chance similarity that may occur; they recognize and name also the drawings, structures, and sculpture of the instructress.

Sometimes they set a goal in advance and draw or model accordingly, although in the actual process they often diverge from their stated goal.

In their drawings, structures, and sculpture there do appear similarities, although distant, to the objects which they name.

Musical Training

Objectives

To develop the child's ability to listen to music and to remember and distinguish special sound characteristics (loud, soft, high, and low); to encourage the children to join in singing, to develop the child's ability to play musical "subject" games and to associate with a given piece of music a general style of movements; to teach the children group movements

The children listen to familiar songs with the melody and accompaniment played on an instrument such as a *mirliton, metallophone,* or piano; they listen to piano songs about the characters in "subject" games ("The Hares and the Teddy Bear," "The Birds and the Automobile," etc.) They join in singing isolated sounds and whole songs with easy melodies and words which are simple in structure.

In musical "subject" games the children play roles and perform various different actions in accordance with the music (for example, the birds are sleeping, they flutter about, and then they fly away).

In exercises and dances the children go from slow movements to more rapid ones, following the sound contrasts in the various parts of the music: they walk and run in pairs, holding on with one's hands; swing around in pairs holding both hands; form circles with the help of an adult; and go back and forth into the center of the circle.

Music Piece for Humming and Singing   "The Hare" and "The Sun," Russian folk songs; "The Shower," music by Vl. Fere; "The Little Bird," music by T. Popatenko; "The New Year's Tree," music by E. Tilicheeva; "The Cat," music by A. Alexandrov; "The Cow," music by M. Raukhverger.

Musical Compositions for Listening   "The Rocking Horse" and "The Mushroom," music by M. Raukhverger; "Winter," music by V. Karaseva; "The Cat," music by V. Vitlins; "From Underneath the Oak" and "The Passage," Russian folk tunes; "The Little Polka," music by D. Kabalevski.

Musical Compositions To Be Accompanied by Movements   Music for Exercises: "Clapping Hands," Russian folk tune; "The Leap," "Stukolka," Ukranian folk tunes; "March," music by E. Parlov; "March and Run," music by A. Alexandrov; "Agile Hands," music by E. Tilicheeva. Music for Games: "The Hare," music by A. Grechaninov; "The Bear," music by V. Rebikov; "Holiday Excursion," music by A. Alexandrov; "Cradle Song" and "The Game," music by V. Vitlin. Music for Dancing: "On Top of the Mountain" and "The Hare," Russian folk tunes; "Stukolka," Ukranian folk tune; "Yurochka," Bellorussian folk song, "Let's Walk and Dance," music by M. Raukhverger.

Music and songs should be heard not only during activity periods but also while the children are doing independent activities.

HOLIDAYS

For the national holidays, the First of May and the Seventh of November, morning parties are organized. For children in this group, a New Year's party should also be arranged; special attention should be given to the children's promotion to the next group.

IV

The Second Younger Group

FOURTH YEAR OF
THE CHILD'S LIFE

EDUCATIONAL OBJECTIVES

To fortify the children's health, strengthen their bodies, develop basic physical skills, teach them good health habits and courtesy, and encourage self-reliance

To develop their ability to play and study together, their respect for their elders, and their willingness to follow orders

To train them to speak the truth; to teach them to express their requests and desires in words

To familiarize them with objects and events in the environment which are within their realm of comprehension and develop in them the proper attitudes toward their environment

To arouse their interest in fairytales, poetry, pictures, music, drawing; to teach them to sing and to portray simple objects in drawing, painting and modeling

CHARACTERISTICS OF CHILDREN DURING THE FOURTH YEAR

The rate of physical development in a child slows down somewhat between the ages of 3 and 4 years. His weight increases on the average by

1½ to 2 kilograms over the year and his height by 4 to 6 centimeters. The child's bone structure stiffens considerably.

At this age further development of the nervous system takes place, but its efficiency is still considerably slower than that of older children.

Mental strain and an overabundance of impressions rapidly fatigue the child and lead to a state of overexcitement. The child's articulation continues to be limited. Although his store of words is considerable, his active vocabulary is still not very large. The child is frequently verbose, but his remarks are usually not very sequential.

If proper pedagogical techniques are employed, the children will relate to their environment in new ways and will engage in more complicated types of activities. There is a significant development in the role-playing games devised by the children. The child's imagination begins to develop. With the help of the teacher he is already able to create clay figures and drawings and structures out of blocks. Later he succeeds even without the verbal instruction of the teacher.

ORGANIZATION OF THE LIFE OF THE GROUP AND EDUCATION OF THE CHILDREN

In the daily schedule the amount of sleep over the 24-hour period remains the same as for the previous group (12 to 12½ hours), while the daytime nap is shortened to 2 hours.

The schedule provides a considerable amount of time for play in the building and outside. It is essential to organize all the routine processes (dressing, washing, eating, etc.) in such a way that they do not detract from the time which has been allocated for play and outdoor recreation. For the outdoor recreation period, part of the group should be dressed and started off first, and then the remaining children are taken care of. In the fall and winter the children have two outdoor recreation periods— in the morning and after their afternoon snack.

Conditioning

The children should be accustomed to having the vents open when they are in the building, and in warm days the windows should be opened. When cold weather sets in vents should be opened periodically for a short time while the children are in the room; the air temperature in the room should be 19–20° C. It is desirable for the children to have their afternoon sleep in the air (on the veranda) or with the vents open.

Dressed according to the season and the weather, the children have daily recreation outside for a total period of three to four hours, except when it is rainy or very cold (-23 to -25° C.)[1] With the room temperature between 18 and 20° C., the children wear light clothing and footwear.

In the summer everything is transferred out into the open air, and it is important to make sure that the children do not get overheated on hot days and that their clothing is light: shorts, sandals, and straw hats. The children should be alternately in the sun and in the shade: in the course of the day, the children are taken out into an open spot two or three times—they play for several minutes in the sun and are then taken back into the shade. The length of these uninterruped intervals in the sun are gradually increased from three-four to five-six minutes.

During the summer the children are sponged daily. The sponging begins with the water temperature at 33° C.; every three or four days, the temperature is lowered by 1 degree until it reaches 23° C. After the sponging the children are rapidly and thoroughly dried. On cool days the sponging should take place in a sheltered spot with the water temperature at 19–20° C.

Morning Exercises

Beginning with the second quarter, morning exercises lasting four or five minutes should be conducted daily. A set of morning exercises consists of two or three drills, imitative in nature and closely resembling games. The exercises are repeated four or five times. On warm days the exercises are conducted on the playground.

Training in the Enjoyment of Work, Self-Sufficiency, Health Habits, Cleanliness, and Courtesy

The development of sanitary habits and manners continues to be one of the important educational objectives. The realm of habitual behavior continues to grow imperceptibly, and habits acquired previously become stronger and more secure. The children should be able to wash their hands and faces by themselves, roll up their sleeves, and dry themselves off thoroughly; sit calmly at the table, eat by themselves neatly without hurrying, chew their food well; hold their spoon correctly, use napkins and wipe off their mouths after eating; take off their underwear, dresses, and shoes by themselves; undress in the proper order, and put their shoes

---

[1]The temperature indicated is for the central part of the Russian Republic. Depending on local conditions, the children have recreation periods outside in even lower temperatures.

away; put on underwear, dresses, and shoes with the help of adults; help each other undo buttons; clean up toys and put books back into place; refrain from arguing in the building and on the playground; wipe off their feet when entering the building; take care of toys, equipment, books, and furniture.

The teacher must instill in the children the desire to work and to accomplish something by themselves. They participate in keeping order in the common room and on the playground; together with the adults they set the table (put out saucers, plates, and spoons) and prepare materials for the activities; they open up the boxes containing the pencils, brushes, modeling boards, etc. With the teacher's help they feed the fish, birds, and rabbits; and under the observation of adults they water the plants in the room, dry off the larger leaves, sow large seeds, plant onions, and water flower beds and shrubbery. The children should help the teacher in cleaning up the playground, gather up fallen leaves, and carry them off to an indicated spot.

The child still needs considerable help, but one should help him only in the event he cannot do the particular thing by himself.

The children should be able to go up and down stairs by themselves, holding on to the bannister, and should be able to open and close doors. It is important to make sure that the children's posture and carriage are satisfactory.

Broadening Orientation to the Environment: Speech Development

In handling objects of all sorts and in performing simple tasks, the children gain a practical familiarity with objects, their functions, and the precise names which should be applied to them. The children are trained to handle carefully things which might break, shatter, or tear apart.

In associating with adults and other children of their own age, the children memorize the first names and patronymics of their teacher and nurses and the first names of the children. They learn to apply the correct terms to the actions of adults and children in the kindergarten and in the family. They express their desires and requests orally. They listen to adults and answer questions. They ask for things politely, say "thank you," and say "hello" and "goodbye" to adults and other children.

The children are taught to distinguish and name correctly: right and left (hands, shoes), near, far, up and down. Their concept of time is further developed: morning, evening, today, yesterday.

The children pick up pieces of information about animate and inanimate nature, learn to observe weather conditions (rain, snow, cold, hot, the sun shining, it is windy), and recognize the practical—the properties of sand, water, and snow.

By participating in the care of plants and in the gathering of bouquets the children become familiar with the trees, flowers, and vegetables found on the premises and in nearby areas and become accustomed to taking care of the flower beds and admiring the pretty plants. On walks and in the nature corner the children become acquainted with the domestic animals and birds and insects (butterflies and beetles) found in their area and remember the appearance and habits of these creatures (how they move, how they eat, and the sounds they make). The children become accustomed to looking after the animals.

PLAY

The child will develop satisfactorily if his life is full of interesting activity. For a young preschool child such activity is encompassed by his play.

In playing, the children perform many different actions and become familiar with new toys. The child's conceptions of his environment are reflected more and more in his play. With the development of the children's powers of observation and their ability to imitate, "subject" and role-playing games become more and more complex. The children form in groups of two to four. Larger groups are formed on the teacher's initiative. Many of the games are still individual in nature. In their play with sand and building materials, various structures emerge (a hill, a house, a garden, etc.). Interest develops in active games involving rules, and the children develop the ability to follow the rules.

Educational Objectives

To stimulate activity and independence; to create a cheerful disposition in the child and the ability to keep himself busy; to further develop basic physical skills; to develop sociability and the ability to join in cooperative activities in a friendly and organized manner; to add breadth and depth to the child's ideas about his environment; to inspire curiosity and observation; to develop speech, thought, and imagination

Morning Play Period The length of this play period depends on the time each child arrives. The teacher's objective is immediately to include each child in the life of the group and to create a peaceful and cheerful disposition for the day ahead. The children arrive full of impressions of events which occurred at home and of the things they have seen on their way to the kindergarten. They will reflect all of this in their play. The teacher should take into consideration the mood and interests of the children and arrange their play accordingly. For morning play, it is best to organize games involving "subject" toys, educational toys, and building materials. The children play individually and in groups. The teacher makes sure that everyone has found an activity which fits his mood and that the games are peaceful and interesting. Before an activity which will require the children to be attentive and remain seated, it is essential to give them an opportunity to move about freely for 20 or 25 minutes. The children play with rolling toys, wagons, autos, balls, etc.; they run and climb around on little walls and ladders. It is important, however, that they do not become overexcited.

Outdoor Play   While the children are outside, the teacher's objective is to develop physical skills, improve perception, and increase and expand relationships between the children. Children who are not very active require special attention—they should be stimulated to greater activity in every way possible. The teacher alternates active and relaxed games, gives the children opportunities to play by themselves, and from time to time gathers them together for short observations or for group games (circle games and active games involving rules). Such games are played in small groups of five to ten or with all of the children. At the end of the outdoor recreation period, the teacher gathers the children together and takes them into the building.

Play in the open air gives the children many natural opportunities for personal contact. They give each other pushes while sledding, play ball together, play horse and rider, etc. It is essential to encourage them to join together in such ways, to help the young children to agree among themselves and to smooth out the difficulties which arise when they are playing together. In developing sociability, games played with the older children are extremely valuable. During the outdoor recreation periods, it is important to provide for such contact between children of various ages.

For the role-playing and building games the children should have available dolls, animals, dishes, carts, and other toys brought to the playground specifically for this purpose. In warm periods of the year table games and educational games are also brought out to the playground. It is important at all times of the year to give the children an opportunity to continue on the playground those games which they have shown a particular inclination to play in the building. ("Kindergarten," "Family," "Driving an Automobile," "Store," and others). Themes for outside games and the ways in which they combine and alternate, as well as the kinds of observations the children make and the chores they perform, change with the seasons and the weather.

The organization of these games is determined by the objectives which the teacher sets before her and must take into account the weather conditions and the interests of the children. For cold winter days the following type of schedule is recommended: As they come out for the outdoor recreation period (in subgroups), the children play active games and role-playing games—they run, sleigh ride, play "Horses," take dolls for rides, etc. It is important that all the children are active and do a lot of moving about. Then the teacher organizes active games with rules for the whole group or for several children at a time (five to eight). In the intervals between games, observations are made (a snowfall, winter birds and how to feed them, transportation in the street, etc.). The children are given simple tasks to perform, for example, to shovel snow together and transport it on sleighs to a given spot. On windy autumn days the children are given rotating toys and windmills. In wet weather games involving a little less motion are organized since the children must play under an awning.

In spring and summer a large space is given over for play with sand and water. It is very important gradually to get all the children involved in this useful type of play, to show them how to use the natural materials, how to vary their play (transferring the sand from one container to another, filling up buckets with a scoop, making "pies" with the help of molds, building simple structures out of the sand—houses, hills, etc.). The teacher should train the children not to throw sand at each other and not to get all wet.

The children play many active games with balls, climb, clamber up and down little hills, and play on swings (seesaws and various types of swings). On hot days when active games are too tiring, the teacher suggests more relaxed games and circle games.

During the outdoor recreation period, it is important to create conditions amenable to the further development of role-playing games.

It is essential to have certain specific equipment for the playground games: a natural hill or a wooden ramp (in winter a snow mound), a little ladder, a little wall for climbing, a log, a sandbox, a trough or basin for water games (or a small pool), carts, tricycles, rolling toys, wagons, sleighs, autos, balls of various sizes, reins, sand molds, shovels, dolls, pails, etc.

Play Following the Afternoon Nap   In the winter the children play in the building for long periods of time. The teacher's goal is to develop diverse and enduring interests in the children.

In order to attract attention, the games and toys are spread around on tables in easy view of the children. The child has sufficient time during this period to play two or three games (role-playing games, educational games, building, etc.). The teacher watches to make sure that the children do not go from one game to another too quickly, and she shows them possible ways of developing their games and utilizing the toys to the full.

The teacher herself organizes games with several children or a single child, gives out new toys, and helps determine what to play and how to distribute roles. The teacher might show the children a puppet show or wind-up toys or tell them a fairy tale.

Types of Games

Active Games Active games satisfy the children's need for all types of movement and give them the joy of personal contact.

Individual games with rolling toys, autos, wagons, horses, and bicycles give the child an opportunity to improve his basic physical skills—walking, running and jumping. Additional skills develop in team games the ability to coordinate one's movements, to orient oneself in space (not to get in the way of others, to go up to a certain point and stop, or to go in a certain direction). Such games as "The Cat and the Mice," "Catch the Mosquito," "Along the Flat Road," "Ball," "Frogs," and others are played.

Children of this age have a great need for climbing and crawling; they like to walk on all fours portraying animals, climb up and down little walls or ladders, climb under gates and under a string stretched across at a height of 40–50 centimeters.

The development of these physical skills is helped along by the games such as the following: "The Hen and the Chickens" and "Don't Touch the String."

Ball games develop flexibility and coordination of the hands. Children play in groups of two and three; they roll the ball, roll it back and forth to each other, roll it through a little gate with the width of the gate gradually being decreased and the distance to it gradually increased, and they knock over suspended wooden pins. The following games are played: "Roll the Ball to Me," "Roll the Ball Along the Path," "Throw the Ball as Far as You Can."

The teacher gives explanations and demonstrates how to play with the toys. She also checks the children for correct posture.

Active games involving rules are repeated several times.

Role-Playing Games   In these games the children, imitating adults, interpret the relationships among surrounding people, the parents' love for their children, the work of the teachers and doctor, etc. The children greatly enjoy imitating the work of adults.

As the children's impressions expand and the teacher contributes her suggestions, the scheme of a game will develop; the children reproduce several related actions (for example, a child loads an automobile and transports it to a construction site). The children begin to reflect in their play impressions of the things most intimate to them. The children play "Family," portraying the way people take care of a child, the routine work of adults, etc. In playing "Kindergarten," the children most frequently portray the musical activities and holiday celebrations.

On the basis of accumulated impressions (observations, reading, story telling, etc.), a variety of games develop. In role-playing games, toys and especially autos and dolls are of great value. The dolls are given names, dressed, undressed, bathed, and put to sleep. For playing with dolls, toy furniture and dishes are indispensable equipment.

The children watch to make sure that the toys are in order, and together with the teacher they wash the dolls' clothing. In this way the children are taught to take care of and preserve their favorite toys.

Educational Games   Educational games attract the children by their colorfulness, the interesting activity they involve, and the opportunity they afford to solve a problem posed by the toy and to check the correctness of their solution. Through educational games, children acquire sensory experience and the ability to play according to rules.

Educational games are presented in a definite order, according to their level of difficulty, beginning with those which involve relatively simple problems: to select objects by color alone (to lower onto a post rings of the same diameter and color, to separate balls of two colors); to select objects according to size (to assemble a tower out of five or six rings which decrease in diameter; to separate large and small balls of the same color; to put together toys and *matreshki*, pails, eggs, boxes, and spheres, beginning with three or four objects, progressing to five or six, etc.); to select paired pictures (toys, fruits, vegetables, etc.).

Then a more varied choice of objects and a more complicated sequence of actions is presented: for selection by color, the children are challenged to build a tower out of different colored rings of the same diameter, alternating two or three colors in a definite pattern; for selection by size they are required to separate objects (spheres, blocks) of the same color but of three different sizes (small, medium, and large).

Finally they are given toys which pose more complicated problems: to select objects according to both color and size (large and small spheres of two or three different colors); to roll balls through gates of the same color or size (for example, the large ball through the high gate, the small ball through the low gate); to build a tower out of rings which decrease in size, while alternating two or three colors in a specific pattern; in jigsaw puzzles to make a picture out of four parts, then later out of six parts (the pictures will represent familiar objects—"our dishes," "toys," etc.).

In group educational games, rules are established for performing actions simultaneously (on a signal all children perform an action at the same time or stop doing something simultaneously). Then more complicated rules are established, according to which the children perform a sequence of actions (in the game "Whose House?" the voices of the inhabitants of the various "houses" sound out in order).

Musical Educational Games "Where Is the Bell Ringing?" "Whose House?" "The Birds and Their Young."

The children play educational games by themselves. The teacher organizes the group games and acts as the leader (she names the pictures in lotto, sets the order for the sequences of actions in the sound-imitation games, etc.).

Educational games require an organized explanation to the children of the content of the rules. The teacher does this illustratively, playing at first with some of the children and then later with the others. After this the children play independently. Each toy will remain with the group until the children have become interested in it and all have mastered the solution of the problem it suggests. Gradually the toys are replaced by new ones which are more complex in their educational content.

Building Games Playing with building materials is of great educational importance. It greatly enriches the sensory experience of the children. The children acquire more precise conceptions of form, size, color, and spatial relations. Their imagination and perception develop. The teacher makes sure that all the children are able to build and enjoy it. She tries to insure that the children utilize the skills they have acquired in the regular construction activity periods. She helps specific children pick out a subject for construction, she shows the structures erected by older children, builds together with the children, and gets them into the habit of finishing a construction project which they have begun. For this group the building materials of *Agapora* and a set of little bricks of all different colors are used.

The children enjoy using natural materials, such as sand, snow, and water, and exploit the possibilities they afford for many different types of actions (filling up something with sand, transferring the sand from one container to another, building something out of it, modeling with snow, pouring water from one container to another, washing toys, floating them, etc.).

This type of play is of great significance for the development of perception. The children become familiar with the qualities of materials (sand may be sifted, it may be either dry or wet, it can be made into shapes such as pies, etc.; water can be either warm or cold, some objects float in it, others sink; snow is cold, melts, and can be pressed into different shapes). Through this familiarity with the qualities of materials, the child's vocabulary is enriched. He develops the ability to use material in set ways and gets into the habit of paying attention to what his friends are doing. In playing with sand, moreover, creative talent develops; the child builds a hill, a house, etc.

In the beginning this type of play consists of elementary operations of one sort or another. Influenced by the example of the older children and the adults, these operations gradually develop in complexity. The child's imagination develops, his play begins to assume a theme, and toys are introduced (a doll walks in the sand garden or slides on a snowy hill, etc.).

Amusement Toys Amusement toys put the children in a good mood and tie them together through shared experiences. For independent play the children are given amusement toys which are easily set in motion: a walking bull, pecking birds, blacksmiths at work, performing acrobats, crying dolls, etc.

Musical Games Musical games are also organized for the children: "The Train," music by N. Metlov; "Where Are Our Hands?" music by T. Lomova. Dances: "The Polka," music by C. Maikapar, Russian folk dance time. Elementary types of dramatization games are also played in this group.

ACTIVITIES

In his fourth year of life the child's speech and his comprehension of the speech of adults develops rapidly and his explanations, instructions, and stories improve. His capacity for voluntary attention, imitation, and memorization develops. It becomes possible and advisable to conduct regular activity periods with the whole group. These activity periods serve as an introduction to group instruction and involve listening together to the stories and explanations of an adult, listening to music, looking at pictures and slides, participating in discussions or group educational games, drawing and modeling without getting in each other's way, group singing, etc. Activities in which the children acquire knowledge and learn new skills require voluntary attention, self-control, and concentration. The length of each activity depends upon the content: drawing, modeling, musical activities involving movement, and speech development games can last slightly longer. It is essential to take into account the great emotionalism and restlessness of small children and therefore to include in the activities various game elements. It is important to keep in mind that when different activities are alternated, the children will be capable of maintaining their attention for a longer span of time.

Orientation to the Environment: the Native Language

The children are introduced to social events and natural phenomena which are appropriate to their level of understanding and which they can observe in their immediate environment. As the child's conceptual sphere expands, his speech and his power of thought develop. The child learns to answer questions; to describe what he has observed; to correctly name objects, their qualities and their functions; and to describe accurately the activities of different people. He learns to use the grammatically correct forms of words, to pronounce frequently used words without skipping or mixing up any of the sounds or syllables, to pronounce hard consonants without softening them, and to pronounce the sibilants and the sound *r*.

The children are made familiar for the most part with the things which are part of their immediate environment. Thus the order of familiarization with social and natural phenomena given in the program is a general one. It must be adapted to conditions in a given location.

During discussions, excursions, and activities involving pictures, the knowledge which is acquired by the children in their routine life concerning their particular group, their playground and household objects (furniture, dishes, clothing, footwear, bed equipment) is made more secure. The children should know the precise name of an object, its purpose, and the properties which are important for dealing with it in a practical way (some objects can break, tear apart, hurt a person, etc.).

The child's interest in the work of adults is aroused. A child should have an idea of who works in the kindergarten. He should know that the teacher works with the children and plays with them. The nurse cleans up the building, brings the food, washes the dishes, and helps the children dress. The doctor cures children, and the cook prepares breakfast and dinner.

The children should have an idea of the available means of transportation in their particular locality, should be able to distinguish the various vehicles by their appearance, tell what they transport, and who works on them or drives them. For example, on a truck are transported foods, lumber (or other things familiar to the children); people ride in an automobile. In the driver's seat or in the cabin of a truck sits the driver; he drives carefully so that he will not run into anyone. Where the children observe things being transported by wagons and carts they should be given some idea about horses (or other animals). A groom takes care of the horse, feeds it, gives it water, and cleans it.

In familiarizing the child with nature, the teacher attempts to broaden his ideas of animals and plants, to arouse his interest in nature and develop his understanding of the beauty of nature, and finally, to encourage a feeling for the conservation of animals and plants. The children learn to describe the things they see and to distinguish and name (in real life and in pictures) two or three domestic animals which are encountered frequently (cats, dogs, horses, cows, goats, household birds). They learn about some of the characteristics of animals, what they eat, and what kind of voices they have. They discover that fish swim in water, that one must feed the fish in an aquarium, and periodically change the water in the aquarium.

Children become acquainted with animals in the course of the year by observing them in their natural habitats and in the nature corner.

The children should learn to distinguish and name trees, flowers, and grass; they should be able to name one or two types of trees and plants in the area (fir trees, birches, etc.). They should know that there are many leaves on trees, that they are green or yellow (the children inspect trees during the fall, spring, and summer). They should be able to distinguish and name several flowering plants in their own flower garden and in the meadows and woods (pansies, dandelions, bluebells, etc.). They should be able to water and take care of the flowers in the flowerbeds.

In addition, the children should be able to distinguish fruits and vegetables by their appearance (apples, pears, grapes, carrots, potatoes, onions, turnips, etc.).

Artistic Literature

It is essential to develop in the children an interest in books, the desire to listen to reading and storytelling attentively, and to look at illustrations without disturbing one another. Through looking at the illustrations, the children gradually acquire the ability to describe what they see portrayed. The teacher encourages them to tell jokes, short poems (four to eight lines), and certain rhythmical refrains from the fairy tales they have heard. For example:

I left grandfather's

I left grandmother's

It is important for the children to recite the poems distinctly and without hurrying.

The artistic material given in one quarter is repeated in the following ones:

FIRST QUARTER

For Reciting to the Children: "The Tower," "Kolobok" (Russian folk tales).

For Reading and Looking at the Illustrations: "The Toys," A. Barto; "My Teddybear," Z. Alexandrov; "Mashenka Eats Dinner," S. Kaputikan.

For Memorization: "The Night Has Passed," "Skokposkok" (from the collection "Rassipushki"); "Let's Sing a Song in a Friendly Way," Z. Alexandrov; "The Rocking-Horse," A. Barto.

SECOND QUARTER

For Reciting to the Children: "Salt, Coal, and Beans," The Grimm Brothers.

For Reading: "The Nursery Garden," N. Zabila; "The Gloves," S. Marshak; "Block on Top of Block," Ya. Taitz; "Moydodir," K. Chukovsky.

For Memorization: "Obnovki," "Grow, Pigtail, Grow," P. Voron'ko (from the collection "Rassipushki"); "The Flame," E. Blaginina; "The Teddybear," A. Barto.

THIRD QUARTER

For Reciting to the Children: "The Three Bears," L. Tolstoy.

For Reading: "What a Mother!" E. Blaginina; "The Ball," S. Marshak; "A Book about Four Flowers," N. Sakonskaya; "Mashenka," A. Barto; "About a Beetle," N. Kalinina.

For Memorization: "Kusan'ka Marisen'ka"; "The Flag," A. Barto; "My Horse," N. Klovkova; "The Mice," S. Marshak.

FOURTH QUARTER

For Reciting to the Children: "The Wolf and the Little Goats" (adaptation by K. Ushinsky); "The Bear and the Girl."

For Reading: "Yasochka Is Down by the River," N. Zabila; "The Chickens," K. Chukovsky; "The Ladder," E. Shabad; "Story about the Girl Marinka," N. Zabila.

For Memorization: "The Cat's House," A. Barto; "The Little Ball," O. Bisotsky; "The Little Mushroom," "Geese, O You Geese."

Drawing, Modeling, Cutting and Pasting, Construction

Objectives

> To stimulate the children to draw, model, and build, and to develop their esthetic sense and their ability to deal with size, shape, color, and quantity

No less than half of all the activities in drawing and modeling should be given over to independent work by the children on projects of their own choosing.

As a result of instruction in various ways of portraying things, the children gradually build up skills which enable them to model and draw by themselves certain familiar objects and to attain rough likenesses.

Each activity must be interesting to the children. The teacher should select a diversity of subjects for drawing and modeling which are appropriate with respect to the season of the year and the specific conditions at the kindergarten.

FIRST QUARTER

Drawing: Drawing straight lines from left to right and from the top to the bottom, and to intersect lines. Typical content of the drawings: ribbons, roads, pencils, rain, fences, cages, etc.

Modeling: Shaping a lump of clay between the palms with straight movements. Typical results: poles, sausages.

Cutting and Pasting: Arranging ready-made forms in a specified order along a strip (circles of two colors or squares), alternating them by color and then pasting them on. Pasting on outlines of various objects (a ball, a mushroom, etc.).

Construction: Copying the teacher in placing little bricks over a large surface and spacing them evenly (roads, railroad tracks). Placing little bricks on a smaller surface and placing them at equal distances from each other around a circle or in a rectangular arrangement (fences, enclosures, etc.).

SECOND QUARTER

Drawing: Drawing closed lines, getting circular forms, practicing drawing circular shapes, and solidifing knowledge of the circular form (balls, wheels), forming oblique and straight lines (a Christmas tree decorated with balls, etc.).

Modeling: Rolling a lump of clay between the palms with circular motions (apple, ball, cherries), flattening a spherical lump of clay between the palms (flat cakes, cookies, etc.).

Cutting and Pasting: Same as in the first quarter, but with an alternation along the strip of different forms of various colors (circles, squares, outlines of various objects).

Building: Piling bricks up flat (a flight of stairs), on their sides (houses, towers), and making roofs (gates, benches, tables, bridges).

THIRD QUARTER

Drawing: Drawing rectangular shapes and succeeding in obtaining better likenesses: books, flags, etc.: solidifying knowledge of the square; coloring in certain objects in their characteristic colors, selecting the colors from among others (green New Year's trees, red flags, etc.).

Modeling: Sculpting simple objects, consisting of several parts of the same or various forms (a snowman out of two spheres, an airplane out of two elongated pieces of clay, etc.); determining the form—circular, straight; pinching the edges of the figure with the tips of the fingers and pressing the pieces together smoothly.

Cutting and Pasting: Arranging various forms and pasting them on in a specified order (circles, squares, triangles of one or two colors).

Construction: Building not only with bricks but also with a variety of materials: bricks, wooden bars, triangular prisms (houses, tables, garages).

FOURTH QUARTER

Drawing: Drawing objects consisting of several different forms and lines familiar to the children (wagons, flowers, New Year's trees, etc.).

Modeling: Modeling large and small objects of the child's own choosing.

Cutting and Pasting: Putting together and pasting on objects consisting of two or three parts (wagons, mushrooms, towers, etc.).

Construction: Building independent structures according to the child's own conception, on the basis of skills he has acquired.

In the activity periods devoted to drawing, modeling, cutting and pasting, and construction, the teacher teaches the children to hold a pencil or brush correctly (in the right hand, between the middle and index fingers, grasping it above and not too close to the point); not to press too hard with the pencil, to put paint on the brush neatly and deftly, to move the pencil or brush along the paper without exerting extra pressure. She teaches how to use clay neatly—not to soil the table or one's clothes, to model over a board, to roll up one's sleeves before modeling, to put paste on the brush neatly, to keep something under the paper when applying the paste, to sit properly, and not hunched over and not leaning one's chest against the table. The children are shown how to distinguish and name correctly the size and color of various objects and the quantity involved (large, small, largest, larger, smaller, long, short, tall, low, a few, a lot, one, two, three); to distinguish and name various shapes (circles, squares) and also six colors—red, yellow, green, blue, white, and black.

Computation

[The purpose of this instruction is to teach the children how to put together a quantity of separate objects, to take away one object from the group, and to distinguish "many" and "one." They are shown how] to discover what types of objects in the room there are many of and which types of objects there is just one of. [They] learn to compare one quantity with another by pulling them up, one underneath the other and learn to see the equality or inequality of the groups and to express this orally. The children [are given] practice in reproducing the exact number of taps or knocks which they have perceived aurally, from one to three, without counting or naming the number, i.e., only on the basis of their aural perception. ("Knock precisely as many times as I have.") It is important for the children to understand and actively employ in their own speech the following expressions: "just as many as," "equal," "more-less," "one by one," "more than one at a time"; to make the words "many" and "one" agree with the nouns they modify in gender, number, and case; to understand the meaning of the question "How much?", and in their answers to be able to use the expression "There are just as many here as there."

This instructional program is conducted during activity periods in the second half of the year.

Musical Training

Objectives

> To amass a store of musical impressions, to evoke a happy mood in the children, to develop the children's ability to listen to music and to recognize familiar songs and pieces; to get the children to sing together and dance to the music, to make sure that the children's posture is correct while singing, and to develop the children's voices

Singing   The children learn to sing songs with expression. They acquire a series of habits—to sing in a natural voice without straining, to hold the long notes in the songs, to pronounce the words distinctly; not to lag behind or get ahead of the others; to carry the tune correctly; to sing songs both with the help of the teacher and alone.

Musical-Rhythmic Movements   The children should learn to move in accordance with the contrasting character of the music, to slow and fast tempos; to react to the beginning and the end of the music; to change the style of movements in pieces comprised of two parts; to execute the following movements: walking in time with the music, running without scraping the feet, jumping as lightly as possible on both feet. Children should learn to perform movements with flags, scarves, and tambourines (raising them, waving them about, striking them), and shift from one movement to another; spring lightly on the feet, squat down smoothly, and portray things by their movements (rabbits hopping, birds flying, etc.). They should be forming circles in games and dances, dancing in pairs, executing dance steps: stamping on alternate feet, stamping with one foot, clapping hands, rotating the hands, spinning around alone and in pairs; performing dances consisting of simple steps.

FIRST QUARTER

Music for Listening: "Lullaby," music by M. Raukhverger; "At Our Gate," Poidu and "L'Ya, Vyidu L'Ya," Russian folk tunes.

Singing   "The Hare" and "Clapping Hands," Russian folk songs.

Games to Songs and Instrumental Music: "The Flag," music by M. Krasev; "Vanya Is Walking," Russian circle games.

Dances and Exercises: "Fingers and Hands," Russian folk tune;

"Walking, Resting," music by M. Krasev; "The Birds Are Flying," music by N. Serov.

Music for Listening: "The Little Fir Tree," music by M. Krasev; "The Doll," music by M. Staro Kadomsky.

Singing: "The Rooster," Russian folk lullaby; "Winter," music by V. Karaseva.

Games to Songs and Instrumental Music: "Playing with the Doll," music by V. Karaseva; "The Teddybear Goes Visiting," music by M. Rauhkverger.

Dances and Exercises: "The Boots" and "By the Street There Is a Sidewalk," Russian folk songs; "Flag Drill," Latvian folk tune; "Dance by the New Year's Tree," music by R. Ravin.

Music for Listening: "The Winter is Gone," music by N. Metlov; "The Pony," music by N. Potlovsky; "The Rain," music by G. Lobachev.

Singing: "Pirozhki," music by A. Filippenko; "The Flags," music by E. Tilicheeva; "The Automobile," music by T. Popatenko.

Games to Songs and Instrumental Music: "The Train," music by N. Metlov; "The Sun and the Rain," (song "The Sun," music by M. Raukhverger; "Etude," music by V. Volkov); "Playing Hide and Seek," Poidu and "L'Ya, Vyidu L'Ya," Russian folk tunes; "The Little Sparrows and the Automobile" ("Spring Song," music by G. Freed, "The Automobile," music by M. Raukhverger).

Dances and Exercises: "Tambourine Dance," Ukranian folk tune, adaptation by K. Kishka; "Let's Go Through the Gate," music by E. Parlov.

Music for Listening: "The Shepherds are Playing their Pipes," music by K. Sorokin.

Singing: "The Chickens," music by A. Filippenko; "The Doll," music by M. Krasev.

Games to Songs and Instrumental Music: "Let's Catch the Hen," Czech folk song, adaptation by A. Alexandrova.

The teacher arranges things so that music is also heard by the group outside of the regular activity periods. On a command from the teacher the children sing out during their games, dance to the accompaniment of folk tunes, and listen to records. For these purposes one may use the following Russian folk songs: "The Hare," "Magpie, Magpie," "The Rain," and "The Billy Goat."

Songs for Marching: "The Stamping Feet," music by M. Raukhverger.

Physical Development

Children in this group must be trained to walk and run with free, easy arm movements, without scraping their feet or lowering their heads, and to run lightly and easily; in rolling balls, to push them energetically; to catch a ball with the hands without pressing it into the stomach; to throw a ball with both hands; to climb alternating the right and left feet; to develop a sense of balance; to jump smoothly, landing with the knees bent; to have proper posture; to stay in place while marching; to perform movements all together, all at the same rate.

FIRST QUARTER

Walking, Running, Exercises for Balance: Walking and running alone, in small groups, and with the whole group in a given direction; to walk one after another (in a column), in small groups, and with the whole group; walking around a circle, sticking to the edge of the playground; walking and running without stepping on lines (distance between the lines—20–25 centimeters); changing the type of movement at a signal (a word, the striking of a tambourine, the end of the music); shifting from a run to a walk, coming to a stop after running or walking.

Jumping: Jumping in place, jumping over a string, and jumping through a hoop.

Throwing: Catching balls (20–25 centimeters in diameter), rolling them back (distance of 1–1½ meters); throwing a ball to the teacher, catching the ball thrown by the teacher (at a distance of ½–1 meter).

Climbing: Climbing under a string or arch (height of 40–50 centimeters) on all fours.

SECOND QUARTER

Walking, Running, Exercises for Balance: Children should be trained to walk in pairs; to walk and run scattering in all directions, in small groups, and with the whole group; to walk along a board placed along the ground; to step over objects lying on the ground (blocks, boards, etc.).

Jumping: Jumping off not very tall objects (height 10–15 centimeters).

Throwing: Rolling balls to each other (distance 1½–2 meters); rolling them back and forth and through gates with a width of 50–60 centimeters and at a distance of 1–1½ meters.

Climbing: Climbing through a hoop; climbing under a string or an arch (height 40–50 centimeters), not touching the floor with one's hands.

THIRD QUARTER

Walking, Running, Exercises for Balance: Walking around a circle holding hands; walking along a board raised to a height of 15–20 centimeters (15–20 centimeters in width).

Jumping: Jumping from a standstill for a distance of 10–15 centimeters.

Throwing: Bouncing a ball against the ground or throwing it up and trying to catch it.

Climbing: Climbing up and down a stepladder without missing any rungs.

FOURTH QUARTER

Walking, Running, Exercises for Balance: Walking in single file, in pairs, around a circle, running one after the other or scattering in all directions; walking along a board placed at an angle (height 15–20 centimeters); walking along a log.

Jumping: Jumping over two lines (distance of 15–20 centimeters between them).

Throwing: Throwing balls forward, sideways (arbitrary distance); dropping a ball placed into a basket (diameter 6–8 centimeters) or into a box placed on the ground at a distance of 1–1½ meters.

Climbing: Climbing up onto or down from a gymnastic apparatus (height 1–1½ meters).

Exercises for the Development of Specific Groups of Muscles

Exercises for the Shoulder Muscles   Raise arms in front—drop them; raise them to the side—drop them; up—drop them; put arms behind back. Shift (a flag or little ball) from one hand to the other; in front, behind the back, above the head. Swing both arms (straight out and bent) at the same time, forward and back.

Exercises for the Leg Muscles   Squat down while holding onto the back of a chair, a bench, or gymnastic rings. While in a squatting position, touch the floor with hands, place an object on the floor and grasp it again. Lift the right foot and then the left, bending them at the knees, raise self up straight.

Exercises for the Muscles of the Torso   Exercises done while sitting on the floor or on a gymnastic apparatus: draw in legs toward you and then straighten them out; turn around, lay an object (a block) on the side or in back of you, and then grasp it again; bend forward, to the side, knock the object against the floor, lay it down and grasp it again. Lying on back, turn over onto stomach and vice versa.

Formations   The children arrange themselves one behind the other in small groups; the whole group goes around in a circle (with the help of the teacher).

Active Games   "Let's Go for a Walk," "Everybody Find His Own House," "Bubble," "Birds in Their Nests," "Train," "Catch the Mosquito," "The Sparrow and the Cat," "The Hen and the Chickens," "Roll the Ball Down the Hill," "Catch the Ball" (individual games with a ball), "Find the Flag."

HOLIDAYS

On the national holidays, the First of May and the Seventh of November, and also on International Women's Day, March 8, morning parties are arranged for the children. The children sing songs, read poems, and perform in choruses and dances. They watch entertaining dramatic presentations and dances performed by the older children.

On the eve of a holiday the teacher takes the children into the street so that they can admire the colorful decorations on the buildings and in the streets.

For the New Year's holiday, dances and choruses are organized around the decorated New Year's tree; entertainment and surprises are arranged for the children.

CELEBRATIONS

In many kindergartens the children's birthdays are observed; the children give their classmate gifts which they have made themselves and congratulate him on his birthday. The cook bakes a sweet cake and all the children are treated to candy. Exciting games and gay dances are arranged for the day.

Three or four times a month the teacher organizes special entertainments for the children: puppet theater; "Magic lantern"; a childhood scene, fairy tale, or an amusing incident; slides and amusement toys. The teacher listens to music with the children, sings their favorite songs, and leads musical games.

V

The Middle Group

FIFTH YEAR OF
THE CHILD'S LIFE

EDUCATIONAL OBJECTIVES

[The educational objectives are] the preservation and strengthening of the children's health and conditioning of their organisms, the further development of physical skills (walking, running, jumping, climbing, throwing), and training in good health habits. The children are trained to volunteer answers to questions, to tell stories, and to pronounce sounds and words correctly; they are familiarized with objects and their properties and with natural phenomena and those events in the life of society which they are able to comprehend. The children's interest in nature, children's books, music, drawing, and building is aroused and cultivated; the qualities of truthfulness and respect for one's elders are instilled.

CHARACTERISTICS OF CHILDREN DURING
THEIR FIFTH YEAR

Further physical development of the child occurs at this age: his weight increases on the average by 1–1½ kilograms, his height by 2–4 centimeters. The hardening of his bone structure continues. The child's muscular system develops and he becomes stronger. The functioning of the higher nervous system improves. The role of his speech in regulating the child's behavior increases. Further development occurs in the activities initiated by the child himself. In the beginning he is not very steadfast in his projects and intentions. They change frequently under the influence of external and chance circumstances, and the child is able to realize them only with the help of an adult.

The children get used to communicating with each other as they play.

They voluntarily run errands, perform tasks, and help out adults. Nevertheless, in order for the child to carry out a task better, the teacher must still relate the task to play motifs which are entertaining for the child.

Increasing the complexity of activities and providing greater depth and breadth of experience influences the development of all the psychological processes: the attention of the child assumes a more stable character; his visual, auditory and sensory perception improves; and his memory develops.

The child's vocabulary increases and his speech becomes connected and sequential. The child's power of thought develops: along with generalizing from the external characteristics of objects, the children begin to identify their most important functional properties. For example, the child combines into a single group an automobile, a carriage, a sled, and a train, based on the fact that "in all of these things people ride." It becomes possible for the children to arrive at an understanding of very elementary casual relationships in such cases where they are involved with events which are very familiar to them from past experiences. More complex moral feelings begin to develop in the children based on their affection for the people close to them. An emotional attitude develops toward good and bad acts. The developing cooperation among the children is still of an unreliable nature and, as a rule, is still confined to play activities.

ORGANIZATION OF THE LIFE OF THE GROUP AND EDUCATION OF THE CHILDREN

The tremendous receptive capacities of children in their fifth year create conditions for the development of enduring skills and habits. At the root of their formation lies the diligent assistance of the pedagogical staff and the establishment of rules which are gradually learned by the children.

The daily schedule must without fail be rigorously observed. One should not make the children wait for their breakfast, their dinner, or their outdoor recreation. The duration of activity periods should be 15–20 minutes; in warm weather they should be conducted for the most part in the open air. Games liven up the life of the children and provide a framework for the exercise of various physical skills.

Conditioning

The children should be accustomed to playing, eating, sleeping, and engaging in activities with the vents open and on warm days with the windows open. In the cold seasons of the year, cool air continues to serve as a basic means of conditioning the children.

The children should be used to being in the room in light clothing, washing in cool water, and spending no less than three or four hours outside daily.

It is important to make sure that in winter the children are dressed in warm but light clothing for their outdoor recreation and that they are kept busy with interesting games and remain active. In winter the children sleep during the day in a room with open vents and, if conditions permit, in sleeping bags on a veranda with open windows. In the summer the whole life of the children is transferred into the open air. In warm weather the children's clothing consists of shorts, sneakers, and a straw hat.

Two or three times during the course of the day the children are taken out into an open area.

Periods of uninterrupted exposure to the sun begin with four or five minutes and increase to eight or ten minutes.

Special procedures for conditioning the children's organisms are conducted under the supervision of the doctor. Conditions permitting, one conditioning procedure is conducted in cold weather—a sponging of the legs and an over-all wetting or rubbing of the body with a damp cloth; in summer, in addition to airbaths, there are wet rubs and bathing.

Sponging the child's legs begins with the temperature of the water at $+30°$ C., and then the temperature is lowered every three or four days by one degree until it reaches $+20°$ C. The wet rubs also begin with the water temperature at $+30°$ C., and this is lowered every two or three days until it reaches $+18°$ C. Sponging the whole body should begin with the water temperature at $+32°$ C.; the temperature should be lowered by one degree every three or four days until it reaches $+22°$ C. or, in the fall-winter period, $+26–27°$ C. In cool weather the sponging should be done inside the building at a temperature of $+19°$ C., or it should be replaced by a wet rub.

In the summer it is recommended that the children be bathed in a lake, river, or pool when the temperature is $+26°$ C. and the temperature of the water is $+22°$ C. The bathing should be carried on for from five to eight minutes.

Morning Exercises

Exercises should be done daily, lasting for five to six minutes. On warm days the morning exercises are transferred out onto the playground. A set of morning exercises consists of three or four drills for various groups of muscles. Each drill is repeated four to six times.

Training in the Enjoyment of Work, Self-sufficiency, Hygiene, Cleanliness, and Courtesy

The 4- to 5-year-old children are trained to be much more independent in taking care of themselves than they were in the pervious period of their lives. They should be able to dress and undress, undo buttons, tie their own shoelaces, help a classmate to undo buttons and hooks, notice when something in their clothing is out of order, and fix it either by themselves or with the help of adults. They should also know how to take care of their clothing and footwear, should not get their clothes wet or soiled while washing and eating, and should put their clothes away or hang them up in place.

The children are trained to wash their hands and faces thoroughly in the morning, before going to sleep, before meals, and whenever else they get dirty. They should know the proper order to observe in washing, and they should know how to wipe their mouths and eat by themselves—take their food in small quantities and chew it well with their mouths closed.

The children should walk and run swinging their arms freely and naturally, lifting their legs and keeping their heads up; they should maintain correct posture in walking and sitting.

The children should greet adults and other children affably and say "good-bye" to them, not interfere in a conversation between their elders, and not interrupt a person who is speaking. It is essential to teach them to ask for things politely and to say "thank you" for any help they have received and also after meals; to wipe off their feet on entering the building and in winter to knock the snow off their boots; to use a hankerchief, and turn away and keep their mouths closed when coughing or sneezing.

Training the children in various work skills and developing in them the habit of making a real effort in work represents another important objective.

Under the supervision of the teacher, the children keep order in the common room and in the playground and participate in cleaning up these areas: with a damp cloth they wipe off chairs and building materials, they wash their toys, and they wipe off large leaves on the plants. They should know where the toys are kept and how they are arranged and should be able to put them back in their places after playing.

Right from the beginning of the year regular dining room duties are assigned. The children set out the plates, spoons, and forks, and distribute fruit. One child on duty is assigned to each table. In the second half of the year, children on duty are involved in the preparations for activities: they bring in necessary equipment and materials and later remove them. The children also perform daily chores, looking after the plants and animals in the nature corner (they water the plants and feed the birds and fish).

The children help the adults in their daily routine work: they get out clean napkins and hang up towels.

In the fall and winter the children together with the adults clean away the leaves and snow on the playground.

Broadening Orientation to the Environment: Speech Development

It is essential to teach the children to name correctly the various furnishings, personal articles, and qualities and properties of objects, fruits, and berries (color, size, shape, taste, etc.); to understand and apply temporal and spatial concepts: today, yesterday, tomorrow, here, there, above, below, near, far. The teacher trains the children to observe the events of nature: "It is raining," "There are puddles on the ground," "The ground is wet," "The sun is shining," "The puddles have dried up," "The wind is blowing," "The branches of the trees are swaying." She gets them to notice changes in the lives of people: "When it rains, they take an umbrella and put on a raincoat and galoshes"; "When it is cold, the building is heated and the people wear warm clothing and footwear." She directs the children's attention to the various means of transportation, explains that people ride in buses and on trolleys, that freight is carried in trucks, and that airplanes carry both people and freight; she shows them streets and houses which are being built.

PLAY

For 4-year-old children a very important position is occupied by games in which the impressions the children have received from the surrounding life and from their favorite books are reflected. To portray what they have thought up in their play, the children use ready-made toys, bits and scraps of materials of all kinds, and building materials.

Educational Objectives

The life of the children is organized in the best possible way in various types of play and games; friendly relationships and sociability develop (the ability to play together, agreeing to share the use of toys and building materials); a cheerful and happy mood is created; and speech, physical skills and agility develop.

In the morning when the children arrive at the kindergarten it is important to organize their activity in the proper way. The child's disposition and behavior during the course of the whole day depend on how and with what he is occupied in the morning hours. Greeting the children, the teacher asks them what they saw on their way to kindergarten and what they did at home. Such conversations serve to motivate the children for play and help to determine the theme of their play. The teacher helps the children who do not know what to occupy themselves with to pick out a toy, suggests someone with whom they might roll a ball back and forth, etc. Gathering several children around her, the teacher plays ball with them or leads a circle game.

The nature of the games after breakfast depends to a considerable extent on the subject of the forthcoming activity. If the activity is going to involve having the children sit at a table, it is better to organize active games; for example, quoits. If the activity is to be musical training or calisthenics, then quiet games with toys or table sets of building materials must be selected.

One should organize the children's play in such a way that their physical and mental capacities are best prepared for the forthcoming activity. Informing the children that the time for play is over, the teacher helps them to make the transition from play to the activity.

Outdoor Play   After the activity, it is appropriate to have active games involving rules and also role-playing and building games which require a large amount of space; for example, playing railroad, pretending to take trips to country homes or collective farms. The teacher alternates active and quiet games. It is very important to organize the children's outside play properly (in the playground), especially on cold days. A gay, entertaining game helps the children to bear up more easily in bad weather. It is essential, moreover, that all the children be able to play. When the children get warmed up, then they go over to quiet games.

Over the course of the winter, all the children should get used to playing peacefully and sledding down hills without being afraid; they should learn to sweep off the paths with a little shovel or broom, participate in team games with rules, slide along icy paths, ski on a level, alternating the right and left feet, put on and take off skis, and throw snowballs at a target. In the spring and summer, games are organized involving water at room temperature in a pool or in basins or troughs, also play with sand in a sandbox. In all of this the teacher must watch to make sure that the children change their positions. Play with sand and water is of great significance for the development of perceptiveness, and therefore it is important to set up conditions for this type of play. Of considerable importance in the spring-summer period is riding on tricycles, both in a straight line and around a circle; swings; and ball games. The children learn to roll the ball, throw it at a target, and throw it up; in addition to making them happy, this will develop their coordination. Playing in pairs, the children get used to coordinating their actions with someone else; they practice throwing and catching the ball.

In cold weather, after their nap the children play inside at first and then on the playground. This time is particularly favorable for building and role-playing games. The teacher helps the children in their choice of games and in making their play a little more involved and strives to teach them friendliness, cooperation, and concern for the younger children.

Types of Games

Role-playing Games The character and contents of the children's games depend on the fullness and sophistication of their conceptions of the environment. The favorite games of children at this age—games with dolls including playing "Family," "Kindergarten," and "Holiday"—are very important in developing the children's sensitivity and their attitudes toward each other and toward adults.

The choice of toys and materials is very significant: the children need dolls of various sizes; toy animals, both domestic and wild; toy vehicles; furniture; dishes and doll clothes. Games in which the children play at driving a car, taking a trip to a country villa, moving into a new apartment, or taking a cruise on a ship will, as a rule, get the boys and girls joined together.

Over the course of the year the children accumulate experience in group games, learn certain rules of social behavior, and get used to the fact that sometimes one has to wait while someone else is playing with a toy and sometimes one has to give up a toy. In supervising their play, it is important to remind the children of the generally accepted forms of courteous address: "Please give me . . ." "May I build with you?."

Common experiences in play bring the children closer together and form in them the habit of being attentive to and concerned for others. Little by little rules start to develop in the children's play, guiding their behavior in a group of their peers. Not all the children immediately submit to the rules, and their violation is not infrequently the cause of conflicts and complaints to the teacher: "But he's kicking the ball with his foot!"; "You're supposed to pull the wagon by the handle," etc.

It is very important to approve the just demands of a child and to encourage actions which conform to the rules.

Dramatization Games and Musical Games   In dramatization games the children act out their favorite fairy tales in small groups.

These games are of great educational significance in that they help to intensify the children's interest in books and develop their creative potentialities.

Musical games are conducted to the accompaniment of a phonograph and singing. Available on records are the march composed by T. Lomova, the Russian folk melody "O, You Beautiful Birchtree," and others. In play periods the children sing and use musical toys; they dance around in a circle to the Russian folk songs "Vanya Is Walking," "Geese, O You Geese," and "The Shower."

Construction   At this age the children play with building materials with great interest. They are taught to think up a structure and select the material by themselves. At the teacher's suggestion and after she has demonstrated the technique, the children build doll houses, tables, chairs, stables, trains, bridges, garages, movie theaters, and theaters.

The children should know exactly what they want to build and be able to make the necessary decisions as to size, shape and color, by following a model or using their own experience. The teacher should encourage in every way possible the children's attempts to make their structures attractive. To play with, the children are given the building materials of *Agapova*, No. 2; the building materials NIII, No. 4; little bricks; and pieces of plywood.

Active Games   In the best active games and traditional circle games, diversion and humor combine with useful movements to develop agility, gracefulness, boldness and self-expression. Active games make the children happy: children always like to run, romp around, chase each other, and run away from each other. Games in which the teacher participates are always lively and gay. The majority of active games are based on obeying definite rules. In games for children of this age, the rules must be simple. The teacher joins in the games with the children and shows them what they are supposed to do. A new game should be repeated three or four times in a row. By the end of the year, the children should have learned how to play several games strictly according to the rules ("Trolley," "Find Yourself a Partner," "Bear in the Forest," "The Sparrows and the Car," "Horses," and "The Rabbit Sits and Sits").

Educational Games Through educational games the children learn to determine the quantity or qualities of objects, to examine the way they are arranged, and to remember them and compare them by their external characteristics. The actions involved in educational games demand definite physical and mental efforts from the child, thus developing his power of concentration, attentiveness, and persistence.

The desire to solve the problem posed by the educational toy motivates the interest of the child and encourages him to fulfill the requirements of the game, which consist of simple interesting actions of a gamelike nature.

In the course of the year the children are given the following educational games: "Who Will Build the Tower First," "Put the Rings Together," "Rolling the Colored Balls," "The Magic Boy," and others. The children are given sets of pictures illustrating objects and animals. They compare them, discover similarities and differences, put them into groups according to a common property, and become familiar with the practical use of various objects.

These games help to develop speed and agility and discipline attentiveness. Toward the same ends, games of lotto are organized; the role of leader passes from one child to the next. In these games, the children's conceptions of the objects and events in their environment are sharpened and expanded.

In educational games such as "Rolling the Colored Balls" and "Lowering the Rings on the Post," the children learn the names of colors. Their notions of size become more precise through games with take apart toys (*matreshki*, containers): the children compare the parts, pick out ones which are identical, and arrange them according to size. The children's general familiarity with the world of objects increases as they play with toys of all sorts, household objects, and pictures in games such as "What's in the Bag?" and "The Magic Bag."

Musical Educational Games "Recognize by the Voice," "Rattle or Tambourine," "What is the Doll Doing?" (the teacher alternates singing a lullaby, a march, and a dance—the child plays with the doll: rocks it, makes it march, makes it dance).

ACTIVITIES

With children in their fifth year of life, one activity is conducted every morning, lasting for 15 to 20 minutes.

In the activities the children are taught to concentrate their attention, to listen to the teacher's instructions, and to act in accordance with them. The children are trained in self-control and discipline (to listen to an explanation right up to the end, to follow instructions carefully, to speak in turn and not interrupt a person who is in the midst of speaking).

The teacher uses artistic material and employs devices characteristic of games for the purpose of developing voluntary attention, perserverance, and steadfastness in the children. The children perceive things especially vividly and learn skills very rapidly when the verbal instructions are not only accompanied by visual aids but are also joined with action. Hearing, seeing, and acting, the children grasp the idea more fully; it exerts a stronger influence on their feelings and makes a deeper impression on their consciousness.

Familiarization with the Environment:
Native Language

Four-year-old children show great interest in surrounding life and nature. At this age they are continuously asking questions of all kinds: "What's this?" "Why?" "How come?" As they find out what is happening around them, who does what, what the objects are which surround them, what they are called, and what their purpose is, the children are learning their native language, its vocabulary, and its grammatical structure.

Before the holidays of the Seventh of November and the First of May, the children are taught poems and songs during activity periods. Together with the teacher they decorate the common room and the playground, observe the way the city is adorned, and take part in a morning holiday party.

The teacher shows the children portraits of V. I. Lenin, tells them that all adults and children love Lenin, and that he loved children and was very concerned for them.

FIRST QUARTER[1]

The children should get to know their way around the kindergarten building (the main hall, the rooms of the older groups, the stairs, the corridor) and know names and functions of various household objects; they should be accustomed to taking good care of things. In educational games involving objects, the children learn the names and functions of

---

[1]Material for familiarizing the children with their environment is supplemented during the course of the year and tied in with observations, the reading of books, and storytelling.

different pieces of furniture, dishes, bed equipment, toys, and other equipment.

In the process of various activities—excursions, discussions, story-telling—the children are familiarized with the occupations of different people (handyman, driver, cleaning woman, nurse, cook, etc.). In observing the work of adults, the children discover why a particular type of work is necessary and in what order certain work processes are performed; they find out the names of various work tools. The teachers cultivate in the children a respect and interest in work and the desire to perform useful services.

The children are given information about means of transportation. During an excursion the teacher calls their attention to a passing bus, tells them that many people ride on it, and that it takes them rapidly to work and to the theater; the bus is driven by a bus driver who sits in a little compartment. The passengers themselves drop the fare into the register. The children observe a train, if this is possible; they learn that it travels along rails.

The children are given information about air transportation and transportation by water: the pilot in the airplane transports people through the air, the plane flies rapidly; people travel by water in a ship or in boats; a captain steers the ship. The children should know the name of the river, lake, or sea bordering the population center in which the kindergarten is located.

Familiarization with Nature

On walks, on nature trips, and while looking after the animals and plants, the children's capacity to observe natural events is developed. Objectives are set: to add depth and breadth to the children's conceptions of frequently encountered animals, plants, and objects, and phenomena of inanimate nature; to teach the children to observe, to lead them to simple generalizations, and to establish obvious relationships between objects and natural events; to instill a concern for the preservation of nature and develop the children's ability to notice and appreciate its beauty. In the course of familiarizing the children with nature, it is essential to increase their vocabulary.

The reading of stories, fairy tales, and poems develops their interest in the living things in nature.

Familiarizing the children with the events of nature opens up tremendous new possibilities for their esthetic instruction.

The Animal World   In the course of the year the children learn to recognize the domestic animals, both in pictures and in life, and to name them correctly (cows, horses, goats, rabbits, roosters, chickens, geese, and all their young). The children should know the habits of the various domestic animals, their voices, what things they do which are useful to people, and what they eat; they should be able to recognize and name two or three types of birds frequently encountered in their particular area (for example sparrows, crows, bullfinches, and doves) and be able to distinguish them by their voices (the sparrow chirps, the dove coos, and the crow caws). It is important to direct the children's attention to the external characteristics of birds (their eyes, beaks, delicate legs, and wings) and their characteristic habits: how they fly up to a piece of food they have caught sight of, how they peck, how they hop around, and how they fly. The children should know that fish live in water, that they have fins and tails, that they swim and catch food with their mouths; fish in an aquarium must be looked after and fed, and their water must be changed.

In the spring and summer the children observe frogs, beetles, and butterflies. Frogs jump around in the grass, swim in water, and catch flies with their tongues. Beetles have wings, they fly, land on flowers, and fold up their wings.

The Plant World   In all seasons of the year it is important to examine trees with the children. A tree has branches and on the branches there are leaves; dry leaves fall off the tree onto the ground. Fir trees and pine trees have needles. In the autumn the children observe the falling of the leaves. The children should be able to recognize and name two or three of the trees in their own yard, for example, poplars, birches, spruces, pines, and others; should be able to recognize two or three of the plants in the flower garden, such as pansies, daisies, and carnations; should know a few field flowers, such as chamomiles, bluebells, and dandelions; should take notice of the pretty flowers in the flowerbeds; should know how to plant bulbs in a flowerbox or flowerbed and plant radishes and peas; should be able to distinguish between carrots, radishes, turnips, sugarbeets, apples, pears, and plums, both by their appearance and their taste.

One should lead the children to simple generalizations from their accumulated knowledge of winter and summer phenomena in nature: in winter it is cold, it snows; in summer the sun is very warm, it is hot, there is lots of grass and many flowers, on the trees there are green leaves, butterflies and beetles fly about, and the berries ripen.

The Native Language

Pronunciation of Sounds By the end of the year the children should be able to pronounce correctly all the sounds in the Russian language.

Colloquial Speech and Storytelling The children answer the teacher's questions; they use in their active speech the vocabulary which they have acquired through the daily routine and activities; they use the correct grammatical forms of words which are inflected. They are able to retell fairy tales and stories which are very familiar to them.

Artistic Literature

Artistic literature enlarges the child's sphere of interests and adds depth to his feelings. It is essential to instill a love for the reading and storytelling of the teacher and for poems; to develop the ability of the children to answer questions related to their content; to imbue them with the desire to recite short poems by heart and to retell stories and fairy tales with expression and animation; to develop their ability to examine illustrations carefully and to develop in them an attitude of affection and care toward books.

FIRST QUARTER

For Storytelling: Fairy tales: "The Cat, the Rooster, and the Fox" and "The Wolf and the Seven Little Goats."   .

For Reading: "The Smart Jackdaw," L. Tolstoi; "The First Day in the Kindergarten" and "How the Children Cross the Street," N. Kalinina; "Striped and Whiskered," S. Marshak; "Who Said 'Meow'?", V. Suteev; "The Vegetables," S. Mikhalkov (adopted from Tuvim).

For Memorization: Nursery rhymes: "Gulen'ki," "Koten'kakotok," "The Kitten," "Grow, Pigtail, Grow"; and "The Sailor Hat," by A. Barto.

SECOND QUARTER

For Storytelling: Fairy tales: "The Mittens," "Bychoksmolyanoi bochok"; "A Story about a Snowball," N. Kalinina.

For Reading: "Short Stories," L. Tolstoi; "It Was Winter, but It Was Hot," and "In the Woods Lived a Squirrel"; "A Story about Tanya," Z. Alexandrov; "The Screaming Girl," A. Barto; "How the Horse Took the Wild Animals for a Ride," E. Charushin.

For Memorization: "The Fir Tree," E. Trutneva; "Childhood," I. Surikov; "Where's My Finger?" N. Sakonskaya.

THIRD QUARTER

For Storytelling: "The Snow-Maiden and the Fox" (Russian folk tale); "The Little Red Hat," Sh. Perro; "Two Hungry Bears" (a Hungarian fairy tale); "How Tommy Learned to Swim," E. Charushin.

For Reading: "Portrait of Lenin," S. Pogorelovsky; "After Spring Has Come" and "Roska Had Puppies," L. Tolstoi; "Know How to Wait," K. Ushinsky; "Aibolit" and "The Telephone," K. Chukovsky; "The Fire," S. Marshak.

For Memorization: Nursery rhymes: "Solnyshko-vedryshko," "Rain, Rain," "The Grass," "Come, Spring," "The Bees Are Humming"; "The Puppy," S. Mikhalkov; "The Little Flag," E. Blaginina; "April Shower," S. Pogorelovsky.

FOURTH QUARTER

For Storytelling: Fairy tales: "Lisichka so skalochka; "The Bowl of Cereal," The Brothers Grimm; "The Animals' Winter," Russian folk tale; "Kolosok," Ukranian folk tale.

For Reading: "The Sparrow," E. Charushin; "The Mischievous Chicken," "Tanya's Pirozhok," and "The New Doll," L. Voronkova; "The Story of the Stupid Little Mouse," S. Marshak; "The Little Girl with the Dirty Face," A. Barto; "What Is Good and What Is Bad," V. Mayakovsky.

For Memorization: Nursery rhymes: "Ai-du-du," "The Round Loaf," "Soroka beloboka"; "The Wind Blows over the Sea," A. Pushkin; "The Bluebell" and "The Dandelion," E. Serova.

Computation

FIRST QUARTER

Teach the children to count up to five, using the proper methods:

(1) Naming the cardinal numbers in order and pointing to objects in this order

(2) Making a correspondence between the final cardinal number and the whole collection enumerated, for example, "in all there are three carrots" counting from left to right with the right hand.

One should teach the children to compare collections of objects, including quantities the numerosity of which is expressed by consecutive numbers thereby teaching the methods of counting: "One," "Two," in all two mushrooms; "One," "Two," in all two carrots; the carrots and mushrooms are equal in number—two each; two blue circles and three red circles, the three red ones are more, and the two blue ones are less; three is greater, two is smaller, etc.

SECOND QUARTER

Teach the children to see the equality and inequality of groups of objects: when the objects are at different distances from one another, when they vary in size, etc.

Teach the children to distinguish their right hand from their left, their right foot from their left, their right eye from their left, etc.

THIRD AND FOURTH QUARTERS

Teach the children to count off, take away, or bring up a definite number of objects by following the teacher's example or in accordance with a number which has been named, this number of objects being counted off from a larger quantity ("Count off a number of ducks equal to the number of geese I have put on the table"; "Count off and bring up just as many fish as there are circles on this card"; "Count off three ducks," "five ducks").

Teach the children to count and to count off in accordance with a model or a number which has been named a particular quantity of objects by feel. Teach the children to count sounds up to five.

Teach the children to distinguish the right and left sides of their bodies, to turn around to the right and to the left.

Drawing, Modeling, Cutting and Pasting, Construction

Through these activities it is essential to develop in the children an enduring interest in various types of graphic art; to develop manual dexterity; to make more precise the children's conceptions of the shapes and structures of objects and of color; to teach them to convey these impressions through drawing, modeling, cutting and pasting, and building; to develop esthetic appreciation and a sense of color, rhythm, and form.

One activity period per week is devoted to drawing and modeling; twice a week the children work on their own ideas. During the second half of the year one activity period per month is devoted to sketching and one to independent drawing.

Building activities may even take place in the second half of the day, during playtime.

FIRST   QUARTER

Drawing: [The children are taught] to convey in a drawing the circular, oval, rectangular, and triangular forms of objects and to name the forms; to draw vertical, horizontal, and oblique lines with an even stroke; to depict familiar objects (balls, apples, autumn leaves, flags, houses with surrounding fences, trees, flowers, etc.); to utilize and differentiate colors (red, yellow, green, blue, white, black, brown); to convey the typical coloring of objects; to depict several objects in a single drawing, arranging them in a row on a horizontal line.

The teacher trains the children to hold a pencil and a brush correctly in their right hand, while holding the paper steady with their left hand; to draw the brush properly; to put sufficient paint on the brush, and to scrape off any extra paint against the side of the dish; to dip the brush in water without spraying the water; and to dry the brush by wrapping it in a rag.

Modeling: The children are trained to roll a lump of clay between the palms of the hands with straight and circular movements; to flatten it out with the palms; to impart to it with the fingers a circular, oval, or cylindrical shape; and to convey typical details (apples, nuts, carrots, mushrooms, columns, sausages).

Cutting and Pasting: The children are taught to paste on cardboard prepared illustrations of various forms (red, blue, yellow, and green circles and rectangles—balloons, flags on poles); to make designs out of prepared forms along a strip, around a circle, or in a square; and to paste the forms on in the proper order.

Construction: After a demonstration and an explanation the children should be able to construct familiar objects with certain details (a bridge with a railing, a house with windows, a two-story house with a staircase). They should know how to distinguish by size different parts and details of a structure (large-small, long-short, high-low); to distinguish among cubes, bricks, and arches; and to name these objects correctly.

SECOND QUARTER

Drawing: [The children are trained] to depict an extremely simple configuration of objects—their forms and the arrangement of the parts (from above, from below, from one side, and from the other side); to convey the coloring of objects, making use of knowledge of colors assimilated during the first quarter (fir trees, leafy trees, houses, doll houses, snowmen). In the winter the teacher attracts the children's attention to trees covered with snow and to the snow piled up on fences and roofs. The children examine snowmen, notice how they are made out of balls of snow of various sizes; they are excited and pleased by the New Year's tree decorated with ornaments and lights. The teacher suggests various themes related to these things for drawing, modeling, and pasting. The children learn to paint or color with a pencil small sections of a drawing; to draw lines smoothly and lightly, not pressing down too hard; and to change the direction of lines by twisting their hands rather than the sheet of paper.

Modeling: [The children are shown how] to model objects consisting of several pieces and to arrange the pieces correctly (an old snowwoman, a girl in a long coat, a bird, etc.); to pinch off the edges of a form with the tips of the fingers; to round off the sides and sharpen the end of a column with the fingers (*pirozhki*, cakes, cookies, carrots).

Cutting and Pasting: [They are taught] to spread out the parts and paste on representations of objects consisting of two or three prepared forms (circles, rectangles, triangles—snowmen, houses, wagons); to paste in a row circles and ovals, alternating them by color (New Year's tree ornaments).

Construction: [The children are taught] to make things by folding paper and to attach certain details (windows, a door and a chimney for the houses, wheels for buses, a back for chairs); to place bricks on their edges, forming angles, and to enclose an area; to build simple structures using various colors; to select the bricks according to color; to build garages, boats, and doll furniture.

THIRD QUARTER

Drawing: [The children are taught] to convey the shape and the proper arrangement of the various parts of objects and to include certain details: placing pictures of objects in a line and connecting them with a unified theme (a house; next to it a tree; under the tree, a bench; a girl has come out to take a walk; the sun is shining).

[They are shown how] to make stripes with a brush, to stroke the brush smoothly; to decorate a strip of paper or a square with a design made out of dots and lines (it is necessary to get the children to turn their attention to applying the colors according to a pattern, to alternate the colors, and arrange them attractively).

Modeling: [The children are taught] to stretch out the clay in modeling the more delicate parts of an object; to press into a rounded piece of clay in order to hollow it out; to turn up the edges of a flat piece, to attach other pieces, pressing them together smoothly and making them stick (hens, chickens, etc.).

Cutting and Pasting: The children [are taught] to hold scissors correctly and to open and close them in such a way as to make a smooth cut and to cut across narrow, and later wider, strips of paper.

Construction: [The children are taught] to choose details suitable in shape, size, and color for the type of structure to be built (a house, a bridge, a pergola) and to be able to reproduce familiar objects without a model.

The children make flags to decorate the playground, tickets for games, etc. For the Eighth of March they can prepare presents for their mothers in the form of paper toys and simple cut-out figures.

FOURTH QUARTER

Drawing, Modeling, Cutting and Pasting: The children apply freely the skills they have acquired and attempt to express their own impressions.

Construction: [The children] build simple toys out of natural materials (cones, leaves, twigs, straw); construct roads, bridges, and tunnels in sand; play with the things they have constructed (play takes place during outside recreation period in groups of six to eight children). The children build buses, automobiles, and doll houses out of large building materials, crates, and boards.

Musical Training

Objectives

> To develop an interest in and love for music and the desire to listen to it; to build up a store of musical impressions in the children; and, through music, to contribute to the development in the children feelings of love for their environment

To develop the children's ability to listen to music and to grasp the mood conveyed by the music and to develop the memory of the children through recognition of songs and melodies hummed or played without words

To train the children to sing together and to coordinate their movements; to perform individually; to maintain proper posture while singing and making accompanying movements; to protect the children's voices by only working on songs with limited range; to repeat familiar songs, games, and dances in order for the children to learn them better; to develop an ear for melody by training the children to carry a tune; to develop a sense of rhythm by stressing the rhythmical performance of movements

Singing The children [are taught] to sing in a natural voice without straining or yelling, to hold notes when singing, to take breaths between short musical phrases, to pronounce the words distinctly and correctly, to begin and end a song together; to carry the tune properly, to sing with and without instrumental accompaniment with the help of the teacher.

Musical-Rhythmic Movements The children should be able to move in accordance with the contrasts in the music, the dynamics (loud-soft), and the pitch (high-low); to move in time to moderate and fast tempos; to begin and end their movement at the same time as the music begins and ends. The children should be able to perform the following movements: to walk gently, spiritedly; to run lightly; to jump a small distance forward; to go at a gallop; to perform various movements with flags and scarves (upwards, sideways, downwards); to make the legs tense and squat down gently; to execute certain figures, to go off in all directions from a circle and then reform the circle; to move in pairs around a circle in various dances and circle dances; to perform regular dance steps; to extend the heel of one foot, tap with one foot, clap hands, clap the hands against the knees, rotate the wrists, spin around singly and in pairs (while walking and running); to do simple dances.

FIRST QUARTER

Music for Listening: "The Hare," music by M. Starokodomsky; "O, You Beautiful Birch Tree," Russian folk tune; "The Horse," music by M. Krasev; "The October Song," music by I. Fomenko.

Singing: "Rain and More Rain" and "Two Deaf Men," Russian folk lullabies; "The Drummer," music by M. Krasev; "October Song," music by I. Fomenko.

Games to Songs and Instrumental Music: "Which of Us Is Good?" music by A. Alexandrov; "Vanya Is Walking," Russian folk song; "The Hen and the Rooster," music by G. Freed; "Geese, O You Geese," Russian folk song.

Dances and Exercises: "Dance for Pairs," Latvian polka; "The Drummer," music by D. Kabalevsky; "Lullaby," music by S. Levidov.

SECOND QUARTER

Music for Listening: "The Bear Cubs," "The Song of the Hares," music by M. Krasev; "Lullaby," music by A. Grechaninov.

Singing: "The Sleigh," "The New Year's Tree," "Let's Build a House," music by M. Krasev.

Games to Songs and Instrumental Music: "The Hares and the Bear" ("The Bear," music by V. Rebikov; "The Hare," Russian folk song, arrangement by N. Rimsky-Korsakov); "Game with a Rattle," music by F. Flotov.

Dances and Exercises: "The Leap," Russian folk tune; "Feather Dance" and "Stukolka," Ukranian folk tunes.

THIRD QUARTER

Music for Listening: "The Sparrows," music by M. Krasev; "I Danced with a Mosquito," Russian folk tune, arrangement by A. Lyadov.

Singing: "The Cat," music by V. Vitlin; "Spring Holiday," music by N. Bakhutova.

Games to Songs and Instrumental Music: "We Walked to the Meadow," music by A. Filippenko; "Blind Man's Buff," music by F. Flotov.

Dances and Exercises: "Holiday Dance," music by M. Krasev; "Dance with the Teacher," Russian folk tune; "Colored Scarf Drill," music by T. Lomova; "The Horse," music by N. Potolovsky.

FOURTH QUARTER

Music for Listening: "The Cat Got Sick," "The Cat Recovered," music by A. Grechaninov.

Singing: "The Horse," music by T. Lomova.

Games to Songs and Instrumental Music: "Tanya, the Happy Girl," music by A. Filippenko.

Repetition of all the material covered during the year.

Physical Development

[Objectives]

To improve the ability of the children to walk and run, swinging their arms naturally, keeping their backs straight and not scraping their legs or lowering their heads; to get the children better oriented in space (able to find and stay in their own places in games and exercises); to help develop a sense of balance; to teach the children to jump lightly, to push off from the floor or ground, bending their legs slightly at the knees; to jump up with a free and easy swing of the arms and pushing off from the ground energetically; to teach the children to climb down alternating their feet; to teach the children to assume the correct position when throwing sandbags in a given direction

To teach the children to form a circle or pair off by themselves

To develop the children's ability to perform exercises all at the same rate, coordinating their actions; to develop proper posture

FIRST QUARTER

Walking, Running, Exercises for Balance: Walking and running one behind the other (in a column), keeping close to the outer edge of the playground or the room; walking and running off in all directions and then at a signal from the teacher (a word, a rattle of a tambourine, the end of the music) finding their own places in the column; stopping after walking and running at a signal from the teacher; walking and running around in a circle, holding hands; walking along a board or bench (width 18–20 centimeters, height 20–25 centimeters).

Jumping: Jumping in place, pushing off from the ground energetically; jumping on both feet, propelling themselves forward (distance 1½–2 meters).

Throwing: Rolling balls (diameter 20–25 centimeters) between objects or through gates 40–50 centimeters wide at a distance of 1½–2 meters; throwing a ball up and catching it; throwing a ball against the ground and catching it.

Climbing: Climbing under a pole extended across the backs of two chairs, under a string, or under an arch (height 40–50 centimeters); climbing along a board and along a gymnastic apparatus.

SECOND QUARTER

Walking, Running, Exercises for Balance: Walking and running one behind the other (in a column) in small groups and with the entire group, around the edge of the room or playground, changing leaders. Walking and running between objects which have been strewn about, without touching any of them; walking along a rope laid out in a straight line, in a circle, or zigzag (length 10 meters); climbing up and down a snow bank.

Jumping: Jumping forward on both feet (2–3 meters); jumping down from a height of 15–20 centimeters.

Throwing: Rolling a ball between objects or through a gate (width 40–50 centimeters) at a distance of 1½–2 centimeters; throwing a ball to the teacher and catching a ball thrown by the teacher (distance 1–1½ meters).

Climbing: Climbing along a board (up and down).

THIRD QUARTER

Walking, Running, Exercises for Balance: Walking and running around a circle, holding hands and changing directions; changing from a walk to a run and vice versa at a signal from the teacher; walking and running along a board which is on an incline (width 15–20 centimeters, height 20–25 centimeters).

Jumping: Broad jumping from a standing position (distance 20–30 centimeters); jumping over a cord laid on the ground; jumping through a hoop with a smooth rim.

Throwing: Throwing a sandbag or ball (diameter 6–8 centimeters) at a horizontal target (a box, a basket) at a distance of 1½–2 meters.

Climbing: Climbing up onto a gymnastic apparatus, a wall, or an inclined ladder (height 1½–2 meters), bringing the feet together at each step and also alternating feet; and climbing down from these things.

FOURTH QUARTER

Walking, Running, Exercises for Balance: Raising the knees way up in walking and running; walking along a horizontal or inclined log (straight ahead—alternating feet, sideways—bringing the feet together at each step); running off in all directions, dodging and chasing.

Jumping: Broad jumping from a standing position (30–40 centimeters), jumping over pebbles, poles, and other low (3–5 centimeters) objects.

Throwing: Throwing a ball, sandbag, or cone for distance, with both the right and the left hand; throwing at a vertical target (a hoop, a shield) at a distance of 1½–2 meters.

Climbing: Climbing under a low water pipe and climbing over a log.

Exercises for the Development of Specific Groups of Muscles

Exercises for the Shoulder Muscles   Hands to the side, hands above head, hands behind back, hands on waist, hands on chest. Swing arms forward and back, rotate them. These exercises are performed standing and sitting on the floor, a chair, or a bench, with flags, ropes and rattles.

Exercises for the Leg Muscles   Squat down, gripping the back of a chair or a gymnastic apparatus; without leaning, do two or three knee bends; raise the right and left foot alternately, bending at the knees; raise up on tiptoes and step sideways, bringing the feet together at each step.

Exercises for the Muscles of the Torso   Twist around to the right and to the left, bend forward and to the side from a standing and sitting position (on a bench, chair, or on the floor with the knees hunched up); bend forward and twist around, holding onto an object (a flag, a ball, a rattle, etc.).

Drills   Children in small groups or with the entire group are to form into a column by themselves and also into a circle and into pairs.

Active Games "Airplanes," "Find Your Own Color," "Colored Automobiles," "Call the Noisy One," "The Fox in the Chicken Coop," "The Wolf and the Hares," "The Mice in the Cupboard," "The Rabbits," "Throw It Up—Catch It," "Knock Down the Pins," "Throw the Ball over the Net," "Fall into the Circle Like a Bag," individual games with a ball, "Find Where It Is Hidden," "Run Softly."

Sports

Sleigh Riding   Sliding down a small hill, pushing each other.

Sliding   Sliding along icy paths.

Skiing   Walking along a level ski track, extending the right and left foot alternately; knowing how to put on and take off skis.

Cycling   Riding a tricycle in a straight line and in a circle, and turning to the right and to the left.

Bathing (preparation for swimming) Playing and splashing around in
a shallow stream, lake, or pool; kicking the feet up and down while
sitting in a shallow spot.

HOLIDAYS

The national holidays, the Seventh of November and the First of May
are celebrated with a morning party in which all the children take an
active part: they dance, sing, read poems, play and watch shows put on
by the older children and adults. The teacher gives the children a chance
to participate in the preparations to the extent to which they are capable.

The preparation for the holiday and the holiday itself must provide
happy experiences for every child.

The children are involved in the preparation for the New Year's tree
celebration; they take part in dances, circle dances and games.

As the Eighth of March approaches, the children prepare presents for
their mothers and grandmothers; on the day of the celebration, they
congratulate all the women working at the kindergarten.

CELEBRATIONS

The children's birthdays are gaily celebrated.

Several times a month, in the second half of the day, the teacher, in
accordance with a plan shows the children slides, "magic lantern," and
puppet shows (fairy tales, short plays); and she organizes concerts with
the children's favorite songs and musical compositions.

VI

The Older Group

SIXTH YEAR OF
THE CHILD'S LIFE

EDUCATIONAL OBJECTIVES

In the older group, work continues in strengthening and conditioning the organism of the child, developing his physical skills, and broadening his conceptions of his environment and nature; in cultivating his powers of observation and thought, arousing his curiosity, and training him in his native language; in developing good health habits, courtesy, and the ability to play and study together in a friendly atmosphere and to voluntarily carry out simple obligations; in cultivating truthfulness, the enjoyment of work, respect for elders, love for nature and for the Soviet homeland, and esthetic appreciation and sensitivity.

CHARACTERISTICS OF CHILDREN DURING THE SIXTH YEAR

The physical appearance of a child in his sixth year of life is distinguished by certain definite features. His body proportions change and his activity increases considerably. Great physical activity is an invariable characteristic of children at this age—they are restless and need frequent changes of position, and alternations in their activity.

They successfully master such physical movements as running, walking, and jumping. The more delicate physical skills involving the wrists and fingers develop more slowly and require special exercises.

The increasing resistance of the child's organism must be promoted through conditioning: the children are gradually made accustomed to longer walks beyond the boundaries of the kindergarten, to remaining outside in inclement weather for longer periods than in the previous groups, etc.

Along with gymnastic exercises and active games, appropriate work obligations assume great significance for the physical development of children of this age. However, long periods of strain and relatively heavy loads must be avoided.

Further physical development takes place, and the child's actions become more and more coordinated and precise.

The role of speech in regulating the behavior of the child increases. It becomes possible, for example, during activity periods for the child to carry out independently a teacher's instructions defining not only the general purpose of the activity but also the manner in which it should be performed. Role-playing games develop further and become more involved. In these games the children portray the interrelationships between people which are established in connection with work. The child's urge to do something useful for the people around him takes on a more definite shape. If reminded by an adult, the children are capable of performing regular chores.

Gradually, very simple forms of study are initiated and developed. The child is able to understand the study goal set by the teacher and to attain it; he strives to find out something new and to acquire specific skills. The broadening of the child's experience and the complexity of his activities influence his further psychic development.

The child's perceptiveness assumes a more purposeful character than that of the smaller children. Five-year-old children are capable of examining a picture or object at length and paying special attention to particular details indicated by the teacher.

The capacity to memorize at will develops in the children. The child learns a particular text by repeating it intentionally. The child's imagination becomes more vivid and rich, but it is still tied to whatever child is perceiving and doing at a given moment.

Substantial progress occurs in the area of thinking. Inquisitiveness develops. The 5-year-old child bombards the adults with questions: "Why?" "How come?" "How is it that?"; he is interested not only in immediate causes but also in the ultimate reasons for events. The children begin to make generalizations about objects not only according to their functions but also according to the material they are made out of, where they come from, etc. As a result of his own practical experiences and his acquisition of logical thought processes, the child begins to deduce things for himself.

Will power begins to manifest itself in the children. They are able to subordinate their actions to tasks set by the teacher, to the rules of a game, and to the requirements of the group.

The more complex forms of personal contact with adults, the group life, the cooperation in games and activities, and the performance of regular chores all lead to the development of new feelings in the children. A sense of responsibility appears in the performance of an errand, a feeling of friendliness towards classmates develops, and the love and respect for elders become deeper and more conscious on the part of the children.

Esthetic experiences also become deeper and more involved. The child begins to notice beauty in surrounding nature and in works of art which are within his ability to comprehend.

In connection with the intensive development of conscious activity in the child of this age, intellectual feelings of all kinds emerge: astonishment, doubt, confidence. The intellectual feelings of a 5-year-old child are, however, still very erratic. The child easily satisfies his curiosity with a superficial knowledge of the object which has aroused his interest.

The development of emotions and will power are closely related to the development of personality. Under favorable circumstances and with proper instruction, the children begin to show respect for the work of the people around them, the urge to be of assistance to adults and friends, and the desire to participate in a common undertaking.

ORGANIZATION OF THE LIFE OF THE GROUP AND EDUCATION OF THE CHILDREN

A calm well-ordered group life plays an important role in the children's education. As the degree of self-sufficiency in the children increases, the time allotted for eating, getting ready for recreation, and going to bed is decreased. The health habits and manners acquired by the children facilitate self-reliance, contribute to the development of good relations with the people around them, and give them the opportunity of participating in the common life of the group. If the teacher works constantly and systematically in this regard, self-reliant habits become a natural need of the children. Training in self-control, courtesy, and respect for adults acquires greater and greater significance at this age level. The chores assigned to the children become more involved.

Conditioning

The vents in the common rooms are kept open in fall, winter, and spring. On warm autumn and spring days the windows are opened. If the temperature drops one or two degrees below normal (18° C. for the common room and 14° C. for the bedroom), the windows or vents are closed, but as soon as the air warms up they are again opened. Never allow cold air to blow directly on the children (in activities and at meals).

In the winter, if conditions permit, the children take their naps on verandas, in sleeping bags, and with the windows open. In the summer the whole life of the children is transferred into the open air.

Several times a day the teacher takes the children out to an open sunny spot for five or ten minutes.

When it is cold, one special conditioning procedure is conducted; in the summer, there should be no less than two.

Sponging of the legs begins with the water at a temperature of +28° C. this is decreased by one degree every three or four days until it reaches +18° C. Wet rubs should begin with the water temperature at +28° C., decreasing it by one degree every two or three days until it reaches +18° C.

Sponging the body begins with the water temperature at +31° C., decreasing it every three or four days by one degree until it reaches +20° C.; after spongings, the children are carefully wiped dry with the assistance of the adults. In cool weather the spongings are not discontinued but are moved into the building or are replaced by wet rubs with the same water temperature and an air temperature of not lower than +18° C.

In the presence of two adults, the children are bathed in a river, lake, or pool, in small groups of four or five and with the temperature of the air +25° C. and the water temperature +21° or +22° C. The duration of the bathing is increased to eight or ten minutes.

Sun baths prescribed by the doctor are conducted under his supervision.

Morning Exercises

Morning exercises lasting for six to eight minutes are conducted daily. As soon as the first warm days occur, the morning exercises are performed on the playground.

The morning gymnastic routines consist of four or five exercises for the development of the arm and leg muscles and the muscles of the torso. Each exercise is repeated five or six times. A series of exercises involving objects (hoops, cords, flags) is conducted.

Training in the Enjoyment of Work, Self-sufficiency, Hygiene, Cleanliness, and Courtesy

The children should be polite and say "hello" and "good-bye" to all the adults; call the directress, the teachers, and the nurse by their first names and patronymics; speak softly; look directly at a person who is speaking to them; listen attentively to an adult, and hold their hands still; they should answer questions courteously, say "thank you" after meals and for any assistance they have received, talk with each other in a friendly fashion, and not interfere in a conversation between adults, and not interrupt them; they should show care and concern for the younger children, sympathize with them (offer them help in dressing and undressing, manipulating toys, playing), and carry out the request of an adult willingly and without having to be reminded.

It is essential to develop the children's ability to use furniture and handle household objects correctly (set them out and put them away, etc.), and to cultivate agility and grace in their actions. While walking and while seated at the table, the children should know how to hold themselves erect, not lowering their heads or hunching over; coordinate their movements with those of the other children, pass by without bumping into each other (in the common room, the bedroom, in the street, etc.). During recreation they should be able without difficulty to jump across ditches, get around obstacles, and walk along boards and logs.

The children are trained to wash up at the proper time; and wash their hands by themselves whenever they need it, without having to be reminded; to dry their hands thoroughly; wash their faces, necks and ears with soap; and clean their teeth at night.

It is essential for the children to learn to eat neatly without becoming distracted, to chew quietly, eat over their plates, use their knives and forks properly, take the food in small quantities, and wipe off their mouths after eating.

With children in their sixth year the ability to dress and undress themselves must be maintained and developed; and the children must learn to take care of their clothes, put them away or hang them in place, cover their beds with a blanket, and fold up a sheet and blanket.

The teacher watches to make sure that the children keep their clothes and their hair clean and neat, that they know how to fix them themselves when they are in disorder or to request an adult's assistance in this, that they know how to use a handkerchief, that they wipe off their feet when entering the building, and in winter knock off the snow and change into their shoes.

It is extremely important to train the children to cover their mouths and turn away whenever they sneeze or cough, to make it a habit with them to tidy up the room, keep the playground clean, throw waste in the garbage pail, and take care of the shrubbery.

Broadening Orientation to the Environment: Speech Development

The children's observations of the environment (during recreation, on excursions, etc.) provide them with rich and vivid material to satisfy their interests and curiosity, to broaden their practical experiences, to develop esthetic experiences, and to enrich their vocabulary.

The teacher encourages the children's curiosity and animation and cultivates their powers of observation.

The child should become familiar with and well oriented in the building; should know the names and locations of all the groups, the doctor's office and that of the directress, and the functions and some of the properties of the kindergarten furnishings (furniture, dishes, clothing); they should know what each object is used for, what it is made of, and how to handle it; they should know the names for the occupations of their parents and of the different workers in the kindergarten, their own surname and age, the names of the street on which the kindergarten is located and that on which they themselves live, the names of inanimate objects and events in nature, and of seasonal phenomena. It is important to teach the children the divisions of the day, the days of the week, and the seasons of the year.

The teacher introduces depth and breadth into the children's conceptions of nature and imbues the children with a love for nature and the desire to take care of plants and cultivate them. She attracts the children's attention to the seasonal changes in nature.

In the fall the children observe frost, changes in the color of the grass and the leaves on the trees, and watch the leaves falling from the trees; they gather pretty leaves for their play; they clear away dry leaves, rake them and carry them away to a particular spot; they learn to distinguish the different plants by their seeds and pods. They discover how people prepare for winter: store up wood and coal, apply putty to the cracks in the window frames, heat their barns. In the fall the workers on the *kolkhozes* harvest vegetables and fruit.

In the winter the children observe how the water freezes in ponds, lakes, and rivers; get to know the properties of snow; set up feeding stations for winter birds; observe their habits; compare them in size and shape, in their movements, voices, and coloring. Together with adults they clean away the snow from the paths, sweep it away with a shovel, transport it on sleds to the many plants and trunks of trees.

In the spring the children's attention is turned to the gradual warming and lengthening of the day, to the melting of the snow and the unfreezing of the brooks and the thawing of the earth, to the appearance of grass and buds, as well as butterflies and beetles, and to the habits of the birds and the appearance of leaves on the tree branches which had been cut off and placed in the nature corner. The children participate in digging up the vegetable garden and the flower beds, in sowing seeds, and planting seedlings.

In the summer from time to time the children observe changes in the plants and the flowers, note the appearance of flowers in the meadow, and berries and mushrooms in the woods, and follow the flight of butterflies and beetles. The children listen to the singing of the birds, the croaking of frogs, and the chirping of the grasshoppers.

During walks on the premises of the kindergarten and along the street, it is important to organize observations of traffic and the behavior of pedestrians, and tell and show the children where the post office, square, and particular stores are located.

PLAY

The themes for children's play at this age are not related only to their immediate experiences—they go beyond the life of the family and of the kindergarten. The children in their play pretend to be construction workers or workers on a *kolkhoz;* they play "Railroad", they sail ships along rivers and over oceans; they transport passengers in buses, trollies, and airplanes.

The children introduce elements of creativity and fantasy as they transform their impressions in their play. With the development of team games, the role of speech increases. The theme of the game is more frequently expressed in words. Words help the children to enter into the role and to unite with the other children. The children now more frequently join voluntarily into groups to play games involving rules.

The children's play goes on for longer periods and is more stable. The children, in groups of four to six, can play the same game with enjoyment for about 30 to 35 minutes. Building and role-playing games can go on for especially long periods. The children are capable of returning to a game which has caught their interest for several days running.

In the process of organized and meaningful play activity, the basic needs and interests of the children and the group are satisfied and an atmosphere of friendliness and cooperation is created.

Educational Objectives

The following objectives should be realized in the process of play: developing the children's ability to begin a game in an organized and friendly fashion, to share the different roles and materials, and to let other children join in; training the children to cooperate with each othei and to follow the initiative of a classmate. It is extremely important encourage and develop initiative, purposefulness, boldness, truthfulness, shrewdness, and organization; to sharpen the children's conceptions of their environment and to broaden their outlook; to develop perceptiveness, thought, attentiveness and speech; to improve the basic physical skills (walking, running, jumping, climbing and throwing); and to develop physical qualities (speed, agility, endurance).

Morning Play

The children arrive at the kindergarten full of their own interests, plans, and impressions. Some of them immediately organize a game and agree on roles, materials, and toys, while others have no definite plans or desires for their play. They hesitate in their choice of games and toys. It is necessary to help organize a game for them, suggest a theme for a role-playing or building game, offer to get them together with some other children, and actually get them involved with some group of children who are already playing.

The teacher should steer the games in such a way that a variety of different interests and themes are involved and so that children while playing will experience happiness and satisfaction.

The character and themes of the games and play after breakfast depends on the subject of the forthcoming activity. If the activity will require the child to remain relatively stationary (activities devoted to the native language, computation, drawing, etc.) then the teacher encourages games involving motion: games with balls, hoops, jump ropes, cups, and balls (*bilboquet*), and also role-playing games based on simple ideas. Before a musical activity period or an excursion, the games begun before breakfast are continued. A few minutes before the beginning of the activity period, the children are reminded to put away their toys.

Outdoor Play

During the recreation period there are lots of opportunities for a variety of children's games on the playground. In this period, the organization of the children's life is aimed at developing friendly relationships between the children, developing their ability to join in games voluntarily, and strengthening their health. The games should be of the kind which will give the children plenty of relaxation after the activity period. It is essential to alternate role-playing and building games and games involving rules. In all active games one should take into consideration the degree of physical stress and attention required. In individual play (with balls, hoops, tenpins), as soon as the children learn a simple form of the game, they are introduced to a more complicated one.

Space should be set aside on the playgound for quiet games, active games involving balls, jump rope, bicycle riding, sliding, skiing, throwing balls at targets, etc.

In dry weather familiar active games involving rules are played by the entire group, and then the children as they wish play with sand, balls, and jump ropes, or join in building and role-playing games.

In damp rainy weather, when it is impossible to run, games are organized which do not require a great amount of space: "Theater," "Circus"; games involving rules: 'Who's Flying?" "Whose Voice?" "Where Was the Sound?"; educational games to develop attentiveness, hearing, visual memory: "Who Left?" "What's Been Changed in the Doll's Room?" "Guess from the Movements What Animal This Is," etc.

As winter approaches, games should be organized which do not exhaust the children but which are interesting and get them warm, for example: "We Are Happy Children," "Who's Faster?" "The Conspirators," etc. After the children have warmed up, it is then possible to shift over to role-playing and building games.

The children sleigh ride, ski, build snow houses, garages, bridges, boats, and mounds.

The teacher teaches the children different ways to build things out of snow, offers vital assistance, and keeps her eye on the children who are sledding, skiing, and skating.

Toward the end of the recreation period, it is frequently advisable to return to active games. The teacher gets the children to voluntarily join into groups of five or six and to play such games as, for example, "Geese and Swans," "Whose Horse?" and "Tag." The recreation period might be concluded with a game involving the entire group.

In the spring and summer the recreation period begins with active games organized by the children themselves. By this time they have already learned games with rules, are able to follow the rules, and choose a leader by some counting-out process.

The level of physical development of the children gives ample scope to games involving running, jumping, climbing, and throwing. Ball playing, jump rope, hoops, cycling, roller skating, and swings all take up a great deal of space. It is essential that the children pass from active games to quiet ones (role-playing and building games). Conditions permit wide use of educational games with flowers, leaves, and fruits.

Play with sand and water is organized. The children build piers, swimming pools, and ponds; float ships and boats, etc.

The teacher makes sure that the children shift from one type of play to another and that the toys and gymnastic equipment are being used properly, and she teaches the children new games.

Play after the Nap

While the children are dressing, the teacher finds out who has played what games, who has finished playing a certain game, who wants to begin a new one, who wants to continue the game he was playing, who was playing with whom, etc.

The pedagogical objective consists in deepening and broadening the play interests of the children, creating a friendly atmosphere, and enriching the esthetic impressions of the children.

The teacher should supervise all sorts of play: lead the individual activity of the child in a certain direction, participate in some games, introduce the children to new games, and constantly guide the interrelationships between the children. Among the many types of games, the most important at this particular time of day are the role-playing and building games, which gradually become more complicated and last for longer periods of time.

The teacher should arouse the interest of all the children in musical and educational games.

The length of the play period obligates the teacher to shift the children after a time from one interest to another, to rearrange the groupings, and to arouse and develop their interests. New interests should also be cultivated. Children with limited and erratic interests require special attention.

When they have finished playing, the children will frequently share their impressions with the teacher: talk about how they played, with whom, what construction they wish to save, what game they want to continue, what materials they will need, etc. The teacher encourages their projects; fosters good friendly relationships, independence, and creative ideas. The children should derive satisfaction from playing together.

It is very important to have a sufficient number of toys, educational and table games, building materials, and construction sets.

During this play period the teacher may listen to music with the children, sing a favorite song, tell a story, look at pictures in a book, or show slides.

Types of Games

Role-playing Games In thematic role-playing games, relationships between children are formed, their interests and imagination develop, their perspective is broadened. The children strive to imitate adults, and in their games they portray what their mother, father, and kindergarten teacher do.

The teacher exploits the child's need and desire for playing with dolls and playing "House," to develop his moral feelings: concern, tenderness, and affection for younger children (brothers, sisters). The dolls become the objects of long periods of care on the part of the children. During the children's play, a feeling of enjoyment of work is developed. When the children play "Kindergarten," this helps to develop their self-reliance and initiative; to arouse in the children the desire to recite poems, to tell stories, and to hum and sing songs.

Relying on the interest of children in the work of adults, the teacher encourages and systematically develops role-playing games. Thus, for example, for playing "Store" the children with the teacher's guidance prepare goods which they have seen in a nearby shop or bakery; model vegetables and fruits out of plastic materials; organize a bakery by assigning the various roles among themselves; play at being clerks, cashiers, etc. The game "Our Street" may be developed on the basis of the children's impressions of the work of a taxi driver. The preparation by the children of toy trucks for transporting bread, vegetables, fruits, ice cream, etc., and of sets representing a street with houses, a kindergarten, and stores also contribute to the development of imagination and to cooperation in play.

In order to realize the educational objectives, the teacher uses the following approaches: she talks over with the children what they are going to play and with whom and what toys and materials they will need. Sometimes the children get bogged down in the development of their game, and the teacher helps them out with a question, a piece of advice, a suggestion, or direct participation; she makes sure that the children get an opportunity in the course of their play to draw and design and prepare necessary pieces of equipment. Knowing the themes of the children's games, the teacher figures out ways and opportunities to enrich their content.

Dramatization Games and Musical Games Dramatization games contribute to the development of expressive speech and physical skills and in bringing the children together through their common interest in books. The children are capable of dramatizing by themselves K. Chukovsky's fairy tale "Moydodyr," the Russian folk tale "The Castle," and others.

With the older group musical games are conducted to singing or a pho-
nograph: "Bayu-bayu," M. Krasev; "Our Guests Have Arrived" and
"The Goat," A. Alexandrov; "At Our Gate," "Vaska the Cat," "The
Raven," "Zhili u Babusi" (Ukranian folk song) circle games; "The
Flowers," N. Bakhutov.

In addition to this, the children sometimes sing and dance in the
middle of a role-playing game, listen to the phonograph, and play on
children's instruments. For marches the following recordings may be
used: "The May Holiday," M. Krasev; "Parade" and "Look What We
Can Do," E. Tilicheeva.

For listening, the teacher selects the particular group's favorite song.

There are also available recordings of dance compositions: "The
Teddy Bear and the Doll Do a Lively Dance," M. Kachurbin; "Doll's
Polka," A. Zhivtsov; "March," N. Bogoslovsky; and Russian dance
melodies.

Building Games   As the building skills of 5-year-old children develop,
they represent in their play with construction materials familiar objects,
cars, buildings, etc. Sometimes structures are specially built by the
children for role-playing games which they have devised. In other cases,
their creativity is only directed at the portrayal of some object, and the
structure is not utilized in their play.

The necessity of comparing details, searching for similar elements, and
selecting them from a large number of elements involves the child in
serious thought and thus serves to develop in him precise visual perceptiveness and the ability to distinguish things by their size, shape, color, and
function.

Putting together a structure out of building materials, the children put
the larger and heavier parts at the base of the structure, leave empty
spaces for the windows and doors, and make some sort of covering. They
build the structure according to a drawing or plan and build carts,
wagons, ships, cameras, pumps, etc. from the designs in the "Constructor" set; they put the various parts together firmly and correctly.
The children try to make their structures pretty. Complicated structures
are within the range of ability of children of this age: ships, docks, piers;
railroad lines, stations, sentry boxes, semaphores; kindergartens, per-
golas, doll slides.

For building games the construction material of the artist Mogilevsky
is used; as well as *Kaluzhny* building material; the constructor set of Polikarpov; and, in addition, snow, sand, clay, boxes, crates, boards, pieces
of material, cord, and spools. The teacher introduces the various materials in a particular order depending on the number of differently shaped

pieces; the size of the pieces; and, in general, their variety and complexity.

In playtime the teacher provides the children with building materials and "Constructor" sets for their individual use; she encourages interesting ideas, stimulates the children's efforts and friendly relations between them; she draws the children's attention to the most interesting structures, helps them to add details, demonstrates specific techniques, and challenges them to build according to a drawing, sketch, or description; in introducing into their play new building materials, she shows the children how to use them, how to put the various parts together, how to play with them, and whenever necessary plays with the children herself.

Active Games   Active games increase the children's love of life, contribute to the development of friendly feelings on the part of the children, and strengthen and develop the child's body. The rules of the game regulate the child's behavior; develop endurance, boldness, and agility; and train the children to act fairly.

The following games and individual tasks are recommended for children in their sixth year: catching a ball, finding a hidden flag ("Put on the Ring," "Ball in the Air," "Even Circle" and others).

Games are introduced with the element of competition between groups of children ("Whose Grain Will Be Gathered the Fastest?" "Snow Circles," etc.).

The children derive fun and enjoyment from active games which are accompanied by words and singing, and from circle games: "Perebezhki," "We Are Happy Kids," "Ivan, Ivan," etc.

In selecting games the teacher takes into consideration the interests of the children, their readiness for particular games, and the weather conditions. As a means of organizing games, the teacher shows the children a counting-off device (perhaps in the nature of "odds-evens"). It is best to teach the children new games in small groups. Later the game is played by the entire group. When the children are playing by themselves, the teacher must watch to be sure that they follow the rules of the game.

Educational Games   Educational games interest the children by the various playful actions which they involve: guessing, finding, telling, and naming. The children, guided by the rules of the game, strive to work out a solution to the problem. There is noticeable interest in the quality of the solution to the problem posed by the game (to make the design beautiful, to put the picture or object together correctly, etc.). In the process of mastering the rules and solving the problems, such qualities as resourcefulness, persistence, creativity, and attentiveness are developed, as is the speech of the children.

Games with educational toys are of great significance for the development of spatial perception and for concept formation. Fine building materials such as tiles and thin pieces of wood are used.

The children learn to arrange them in space and to name correctly the place where they have put them (on top, on the bottom, on the side, in the middle, etc.). Games with simple rules are of basic importance (picking out pairs of pictures according to their subjects, where the identical objects have been arranged differently; assembling the parts of something into a whole). The success of these games depends on the children having sufficient knowledge of the phenomena of nature and the work of adults and on their ability to classify objects (by their qualities and functions, by the relation of the parts to the whole, etc.).

These games are conducted at a moderate tempo; they develop attentiveness, contribute to speech development, sharpen spatial perceptions and spatial concepts, etc. ("Store," "Select the Pair," "Colored Dishes," "Put the Picture Together," "How Many to Each One," "We Are Counting," "Who Does What," "To Each One What He Needs," "Zoological Lotto," "It Grows, It Flowers, It Ripens," jigsaw puzzles, "Colored and Geometrical Tiles," "Lotto," "Dominoes," "Catch a Frog in the Swamp," "Tenpins," etc.).

The teacher, taking into consideration the individual characteristics of the children and the opportunities which will be provided for the children to join into groups on their own, distributes various table games to the children for free use. For new games, a brief explanation is given, in some cases supplemented by a demonstration of the rules of the game; the teacher herself plays with the children. In independent games she watches to see that the children follow the rules and arouses the general interest in the games.

Musical educational games are recommended for the older group: "Loud-Soft," "Which Drum Is Playing" (high-low), "Story with Musical Riddles."

WORK

Children in their sixth year are interested in work, and their attitude toward it is positive. They begin to understand its social significance, and they distinguish work from play. Interest in the process of work is tied up with the urge to obtain a definite result. The children are capable of performing simple chores for the common good. They develop the urge to help their friends. Work habits and skills are continually being accumulated.

The teacher arouses in the children an interest in and love for work; she gets them accustomed to performing tasks carefully and voluntarily, to working neatly, taking care of tools and putting them back after the work is over; she cultivates resourcefulness and the ability to pursue a goal conscientiously; she gets them used to performing work for the whole group; she develops collective work patterns (housework, work related to cultivation of the plants and care of the animals) and the habit of checking the work which has been done; she instills in the children a feeling of concern for the plants and animals (in the nature corner and in the kindergarten yard); she endeavors to form proper habits in all types of work and along the way gives the children knowledge about the objects of everyday life, about work and about nature, and encourages a feeling of happiness and satisfaction in work.

Self-service

Work duties provide the opportunity to give the children planned systematic practice in various types of work activity, to develop work habits, and to mould behavior.

The children on duty should know which dishes to set out for breakfast and dinner and should be able to put out dishes with bread; set out the knives, forks, and spoons; serve the third course during the dinner; and crumb the table after the meal. They should be able to work without becoming distracted.

Before the activity periods, it is their duty to prepare the table, to spread out the materials and equipment, and, later, to put them away in their places; to wash brushes, glasses, and paint dishes; to scour trays used in pasting and painting; and to wipe off the tables with a damp cloth after modeling.

In the nature corner the children on duty water the plants and dust or wipe off the large leaves. Under the supervision of the teacher they feed the birds and animals, wash off the feeding stations and bird baths, cut vegetables, bring water and grain, fill up and change the water in the fish tank, and sift oats for the birds.

In the course of fulfilling their work duties, the children learn to observe and to comprehend the relationship between the proper care of plants and animals and their condition or health.

Routine Housework

The children participate in the daily cleaning of the common rooms: they dust off the furniture, they wash off celluloid and rubber toys and building materials, and they clean and press the dolls' clothing; in the summer they wash vegetables for lettuce and mixed salads.

Cultivation of the Plants

The children observe the work of adults in the vegetable and flower gardens and in the field. Together with the adults they weed and water the vegetable and flower gardens. The children participate in turning over the earth the second time for flower beds and borders, they plant and water flowers, pick out the obvious weeds and grass, and gather vegetables and seeds.

The children must be taught how to use a shovel, a trowel, rakes, and watering cans.

In the course of the work the children observe changes in the height of the plants and learn to distinguish them by their coloring, fragrance, and appearance.

Handicraft

The children learn to make simple things out of cardboard, plywood, and fir cones (binoculars, flags, satchels, scales, cars, New Year's Tree decorations). For the Eighth of March they make gifts: bookbags, little boxes, pin cushions, and memorandum books. In the course of the work the children get familiar with materials and their properties. The teacher chooses tools and equipment, helps the children to share among themselves the various tasks, demonstrates work techniques, trains them to perform work without bothering each other, promotes friendly relations and cooperation, and strives to develop diligence and industry. Working together in small groups is recommended typically once a week (in the afternoon).

ACTIVITIES

In the activity periods the children develop the ability to work in accordance with the instructions of the teacher. The teacher addresses questions to the children, making more vivid in their memory the things they have previously seen, heard, and observed; she encourages them to express themselves and supplies answers to the questions. The children learn to respond to the teacher's questions, with both short and long answers, and to express their thoughts clearly: to finish a sentence, not leaving out any of the words needed to convey the meaning properly, to use the correct terms for things, and to use the correct inflections and endings for nouns, verbs, etc.

The teacher continues to develop the children's ability to appreciate work; she endeavors to form the habit of working carefully and finishing something which has been started; she teaches the children to be kind and affable and watches to make sure that the children's posture and bearing during active periods is correct. Game techniques are widely utilized. Through repetition the children master skills better and acquire knowledge more readily.

Every day two activities are conducted: the first lasting 25 to 35 and the second, 15 to 20 minutes; in the spring and summer only one activity is conducted.

Familiarization with the Environment; Native Language

Relying on the sensory experience and the observations of the children, the teacher must enrich their concrete notions of physical reality and correspondingly expand their vocabulary (words related to the work of people, to plants, animals, and inanimate nature). She must develop in the children a love for their native area (city, town, or village) and respect for the work of the people around them. In the activity periods preceding the celebrations of the Seventh of November and the First of May, she rehearses poems and songs with the children. The teacher shows the children portraits of V. I. Lenin, tells them about Lenin and about how he loved children and was very concerned for their welfare.

FIRST QUARTER

What Happens in Nature: In the sky there are clouds. It has become cold. The leaves on the trees have turned yellow and then red. The flowers and grass are withering. The butterflies and beetles have disappeared. The birds (rooks, starlings) gather into flocks and fly away to warmer places.

Harvesting Vegetables and Caring for Domestic Animals: The workers on the *kolkhoz* pick potatoes, vegetables (carrots, cabbages, sugar beets, onions); fruits (apples, pears, plums, grapes). On the *kolkhozes* there are cows, horses, sheep, pigs, geese, hens (depending, of course, on local conditions).

The children should be able to name characteristic features in the appearance of domestic animals (cats, dogs, cows, goats, horses, sheep, pigs, hens, geese, ducks, rabbits) and to relate some of these animals to their habits and movements; they should know the benefits to man of the various domestic animals, and how man takes care of them. The process of familiarizing the children with the domestic animals is carried on over the course of the whole year.

Preparation of Food: Soup, borsch, cutlets, stew, lettuce and mixed salads, and other dishes are prepared from vegetables and meat. The cook prepares the food. He works in the kitchen, tries to have everything tasty and ready in time, grills things in large saucepans and fries food in frying pans. In the kitchen it is clean and orderly. The cook works in a white apron (overalls), with a white hat or three-cornered neckerchief. On an excursion to the kitchen with the children, the cook talks with them about how food is prepared.

Anniversary Day of the Great October Socialist Revolution: This holiday is celebrated by all Soviet people. For the holiday, houses, streets, schools, and kindergartens are all decorated with red flags. Adults take part in demonstrations. In the kindergarten morning parties are given.

SECOND QUARTER

What Happens in Nature: It is cold, the water in puddles, in the river (lake, ponds) has frozen and turned into ice. The ice is solid and slippery. One may walk or skate over the ice. On the branches of the trees there are pods, but no leaves. On the branches of pines and spruces there are green needles. The birds are cold and hungry in the winter. They fly up to the houses seeking food. The birds must be fed.

The children examine birds in nature and in pictures and learn the names of several of the birds indigenous to the particular area which fly around the schoolyard; crows, sparrows, goldfinches, and bluebirds. They examine pictures and name wild animals: bears, foxes, wolves, hares, porcupines, squirrels, tigers, lions, elephants, and monkeys. They should know where these animals live and some of their habits. (The process of familiarizing the children with wild animals goes on all during the year.)

People wear warm clothing in winter and their homes are heated. Cattle are kept inside in the winter.

Sewing Clothes: There is summer clothing, fall clothing, and winter clothing. Tailors and dressmakers sew dresses, suits, coats, shirts, etc. They sew materials on sewing machines. For sewing one needs needles, threads, thimbles, buttons, and scissors. Tailors sew carefully so that the clothes will be attractive and comfortable. Everyone likes to wear clothing which is expertly sewn.

The children watch as somebody on the staff or one of the parents sews underwear or children's clothing, and then they themselves sew clothes for the dolls.

The children name characteristic properties of clothing and footwear: color, size, estimates of quality (new, attractive, clean), material (fur, leather). They know the words for general categories: clothing, footwear, etc.

How People Get News about Each Other: People write letters to each other and send telegrams. In these people tell about their health and send greetings on holidays. For a letter, one needs paper, an envelope, and a stamp. These are bought in a post office or in a kiosk. On the envelope one writes the address—the name of the city, the name of the street, the house number, and the surname. Then one attaches the stamp and drops the letter in a mailbox. A mailman delivers letters. He has a large sack of letters. By the address on the envelope he knows to whom a letter should be delivered. Everyone must know his own address.

THIRD QUARTER

What Happens in Nature: The sun gets hotter, the snow and ice melt from the heat, and the streams flow. In the rivers, lakes, and ponds, the ice breaks up and water appears. People plant trees and bushes on the streets and in gardens; in the field they sow wheat, oats, and flax; in their gardens they plant vegetables. Buds appear on the trees and little downy leaves emerge from the buds. The children should be able to distinguish two or three kinds of trees in their school yard: poplars, maples, linden trees, oaks, pines, spruces, etc. Bees, butterflies, caterpillars, and May beetles appear. The caterpillars and May beetles eat leaves.

Children should know the appearance of May beetles (brown, short, fat, and with hard wings) and how they fly and crawl; they should be able to recognize and name one or two types of butterflies (white mushroom butterflies, nettle butterflies, lemon-tree butterflies, and others).

In the spring grasshoppers, swallows, and rooks arrive.

The Twenty-second of April: Birthday of V. I. Lenin: The children together with the adults celebrate this day. They know that V. I. Lenin was always concerned for the welfare of the Soviet people and for children, whom he greatly loved. Everybody remembers and loves Lenin.

How Houses Are Built: Workers build houses out of various types of materials: bricks, panels, cement blocks, logs, and boards. They install electrical wiring and heating. Around the house they plant trees and make walks. It is pleasant for adults and children alike to have the chance to live in a new house.

What People Ride On: People ride and transport things on trains, in automobiles, on buses, on planes, on trolleys, and on bicycles. A locomotive is driven by an engineer, a plane is navigated by a pilot, a bus is driven by a bus driver, and a train by a conductor. People ride from villages to cities and from one city to another.

The children should know the sights and landmarks of their native city or village and the means of transportation. They should be able to name the various types of city transportation.

For the Eighth of March, the children make presents to give their parents on the holiday.

FOURTH QUARTER

What Happens in Nature: In the summer the sun rises early, the day is long and hot, and sometimes there is thunder and it rains.

In the woods, parks, and gardens there are many leaves on the trees; in the woods there are many berries and mushrooms (the children should know the names of the kind of mushrooms used for food). In the meadow, grass and flowers are abundant (they should know and be able to name correctly four or five of the plants in the meadow).

Workers on the *kolkhoz* cut the grass in the fields with scythes, dry it and store the hay away until winter when it will be used to feed the animals. In the fields rye, oats, corn, wheat, and flax are raised. They are harvested by machines. In the vegetable garden the ground is broken, the weeds are pulled out, the soil is fertilized, and the vegetables grow well.

In the river (pond, lake) the water is warm and people bathe and go fishing and boating.

Native Language

As the children gather ideas and form conceptions of their surroundings, their vocabulary expands and is put to more active use.

FIRST QUARTER

[The children are taught] to convey the gist of a literary text with the help of questions from the teacher; to retell familiar fairy tales and the short stories of L. N. Tolstoy.

To recite poems from memory with expression; to speak distinctly and correctly in accordance with the standards of Russian literary pronunciation.

[The child learns] to describe . . . well [enough] to be understood by those listening what he has just observed, what he has just done, or what is illustrated in a picture; to invent descriptive stories using words in their proper grammatical forms.

In reciting from memory or telling stories to convey the intonation of a question, answer, or exclamation; to speak distinctly at a slow and at a more rapid pace.

[The children are encouraged] to invent stories about what is illustrated in a picture; to convey a literary text in a sequential fashion without the aid of questions from the teacher; to read poems, tell fairy tales, and retell short stories by L. N. Tolstoy, K. D. Ushinsky, and Soviet writers.

To speak loudly and softly, while maintaining distinct pronunciation.

[The children should be able] to tell connected stories about events and life at home and in the kindergarten.

To develop further skill in reciting from memory and telling stories expressively; to control loudness of voice and to make use of different tempos of speech.

Artistic Literature

Books broaden a child's perspective, help him to evolve moral principles and lead him beyond immediate experiences.

Children in their sixth year develop the ability to answer questions on the contents and illustrations of a text and the ability to comprehend the highly expressive language of traditional fairy tales, stories, and poems.

For Storytelling: "Geese and Swans;" "The Boastful Hare," Russian fairy tale, adapted by A. Tolstoy.

For Reading: "The Brave Little Duck," B. Zhitkov; "The Little Ones," N. Kalinina; "The Hen and the Golden Egg," A. Donchenko;

"The Live Hat," N. Nosov; "Confusion" and "The Stolen Sun," K. Chukovsky; "The Fire Dogs," L. Tolstoy.

For Memorization: "October Holiday," O. Vysotskaya; "The Trumpeter," S. Marshak; "Autumn" ("Autumn has come ..."), A. N. Pleshcheev.

SECOND QUARTER

For Storytelling: "The Fox and the Gray Wolf," "The Goat," and "The Tails."

For Reading: "The Ignorant One," Y. Akim; "Let's Go to Work," M. Poznanskaya; "Father Steppe," S. Mikhalkov; "On the Mountain," N. Nosov; "Mill-cakes and Cottage Cheese," "How Tanya Picked Out a New Year's Tree," and others from the book "The Snow Is Falling," L. Voronkova.

For Memorization: "The New Year's Tree," "January," S. Marshak; "Andrushka," S. Mikhalkov; "The First Snowfall," I. Surikov; "Snow on the Roof," E. Trutneva.

THIRD QUARTER

For Storytelling: "The Winged One, the Shaggy One, and the Greasy One"; "Kroshechka-Khavroshechka"; "The Geese," traditional Russian fairy tale; "The Musicians from Bremen," fairy tale by the Brothers Grimm.

For Reading: "Let's Sit in Silence," E. Blaginina; "What I Saw" (selected chapters), B. Zhitkov; "The Post Office," S. Marshak; "In the Forest Meadow," G. Skrebitsky; "The String," A. Barto; "The Boy and Lenin," A. Kononov.

For Memorization: "May" and "Spring Song," S. Marshak; "Portrait of Lenin," S. Pogorelovsky; "The Grass Is Growing Green," A. Pleshcheev; "In May," V. Maikov.

FOURTH QUARTER

For Storytelling: "Zhikharka," Russian folk tale; "The Piper and the Jug," V. Kataev; "Visiting the Sun," Slovak fairy tale.

For Reading: "Sunny Day" (selected chapters), L. Voronkova; "Little Children in a Cage," "The Attic," "Look at the Absentminded One," S. Marshak; "Fedor's Grief," K. Chukovsky; "The Bear Cubs," E. Charushin; "What I Saw" (selected chapters), B. Zhitkov.

For Memorization: "June," "July," "August," S. Marshak; "The Brave Ones" and "The Chicken," English folk songs, K. Chukovsky; "The Housepainters," M. Pozharova; "The Linden Tree," P. Voron'ko; "A Pine Grows in Front of the Palace" and "In the Rosy Dawn," A. Pushkin.

Computation

FIRST QUARTER

[*Objectives*]

To teach the children to differentiate and enumerate quantities of objects numbering two and three, three and four, and four and five, on the basis of a comparison of the two quantities of objects; to count off objects up to five, with a model and in response to an indicated number. To be able to take away objects in a deliberate way, one by one, counting along, clearly making the correspondence between a number and every object removed, and defining the last number as the sum total. To be able to discover the relationship between a number and a quantity of objects, regardless of their particular qualities or their arrangement

To be able to count up to five sounds by ear and to be able to count off an indicated quantity of objects by feel.

To be able to distinguish the right and left sides of one's body, and to make right and left turns.

SECOND QUARTER

[*Objectives*]

To teach the children to count and enumerate quantities of objects up to ten on the basis of a comparison of one group of objects with another (i.e., one-to-one), where the groups are represented numerically by consecutive numbers. To develop further skill in recognizing quantities up to ten, with a model and in response to a given number. To be able to perceive numerical equality in groups of different objects and to make correct generalizations (here the number of objects in each group is three, nine, etc.).

To distinguish on a plane surface the left, the right, the upper and the lower sides, the right or left, upper and lower angles, the middle

THIRD QUARTER

[*Objectives*]

To teach the child to recognize quantities of objects up to ten, to perceive by ear a quantity of sounds, to count a quantity of objects by feel, to repeat actions of various types a specified number of times (bounce a ball "x" times, etc.)

To be able to group objects corresponding in quantity to the numbers from one to five

To be able to compare consecutive numbers, relying on concrete materials, and to know how to make an equality from an inequality (five is greater than four, if one is added to four, you get five, and the quantities are equal in number; four is less than five, here there is one too few, and if one is taken away from five then there will be four in each group, and the quantities will be equal in number)

To teach the children to count, using the first five ordinal numbers; to differentiate between questions which must be answered by ordinal number and those which must be answered by a cardinal number

FOURTH QUARTER

Review of the material already covered.

Drawing and Painting, Modeling, Cutting and Pasting, Construction

In these activities, powers of observation and esthetic sensitivity are developed; more precise conceptions are formed of the shapes of objects and their differences and similarities, of the relative positions of their parts, of their relative sizes and their characteristic features, and of the coloring of objects. The children develop artistic taste—they are able to select colors which will go well together, to arrange the shapes in a design or the parts of a structure symmetrically, to put together a pretty ornament, to decorate modeled figures and paper objects. Their imagination develops, as do their self-reliance, initiative, resourcefulness, and ability to concentrate.

FIRST QUARTER

Drawing and Painting: The children learn to convey the basic shape of objects and their parts by relying on a knowledge of forms: circles, ovals, rectangles, triangles, the relative size of objects and their arrangement; to convey the coloring of objects by relying on a knowledge of the colors: red, orange, yellow, green, blue, violet, black, white, and brown; to select colors which according to their taste go well together.

The children paint from nature flowers, fruits, vegetables, and toys; after observations made during a walk, they paint trees with autumn leaves, houses, trolleys, and buses.

In their paintings the children reflect their rich impressions of the October holiday.

On a square piece of paper the children make symmetrical designs out of lines, dots, spots, and circles; they learn to distinguish the middle, the angles, and the upper, lower, right, and left sides.

Certain habits must be developed in drawing: not to press too hard on the pencil; to hold it slanted; to make even strokes with a light movement in a particular direction, back and forth.

In painting, the children learn to saturate the end of the brush with paint; to hold the brush vertically when making lines, but in painting over an area to hold it on a slant, moving it always in one direction, i.e., from left to right, from top to bottom, or diagonally. These skills are developed throughout the course of the year.

Modeling: The children model simply shaped objects out of clay and plastic materials (vegetables, fruits) and' also more complicated ones (certain animals, dolls). In order to convey the characteristic features of various different shapes, actions requiring all parts of the hands, and especially the fingers, must be utilized: rolling, flattening, pressing in, stretching out, pinching, and smoothing.

Cutting and Pasting: The children learn to cut paper in a straight line, gradually lengthening the cut, and to make slanted cuts; in this way they obtain squares, triangles and trapezoids (houses, boats, flags). Circular shapes are given to the children ready-made.

Construction: The children are taught to see the main features in a model structure, to be able to copy them and arrange the various parts of the structure symmetrically. Folding a piece of paper in half, the children match up the edges of the paper (preparation of an album); they learn to fold the paper into four parts and to make the folds even. They paste together small lanterns and other toys.

SECOND QUARTER

Drawing and Painting: The children learn to convey differences in size and to give the right proportions to objects: tall-small, narrow-wide (a tall New Year's tree and a small one, a tall house, a low hut). They learn how to depict in a drawing or painting several objects related by a common theme (a picture of nature; an event from surrounding life; the subject of a fairy tale, story, poem, or song: "A Fir Tree Was Born in the Forest," "Two Hungry Bear Cubs"). In their paintings they reflect their impressions of the New Year's celebration: the children paint a New Year's tree with toys and some of the figures associated with the celebration of the New Year. In decorative paintings, the children make designs on circles, diamonds, and hexagons and convey the idea of a snowflake. It is important to teach the children to move the end of the brush along lightly and confidently in making straight, curved, and wavy lines, circles, arcs and dots; and to hold the stem of the brush up vertically.

Modeling: The children learn to convey basic characteristics of objects: long and short, fat and thin; to set their figures up in a vertical position, to convey the proper relative sizes of the parts, to secure solidly the various parts of a figure which they have modeled by pressing them up against each other and smoothing over the places where the parts have been joined (snowmen, boys on sleighs, hares, dogs, teddy bears, etc.). They learn to model objects out of a single piece.

Cutting and Pasting: The children learn to cut in a straight line and to cut out circles and oval shapes from rectangles (vegetables, snowmen, etc.); they learn to round off angular edges (airplanes, towers made out of different sized rings joined together), and they learn to make secure symmetric designs out of geometrical shapes.

Construction: The children make stable models of increasing complexity (a street, a zoo, a station, a *kolkhoz,* etc.); and in making their models, they utilize the subjects of fairy tales.

One should teach the children to make toys without any pasting by folding rectangular pieces of paper and also to make an object by following a pattern.

THIRD QUARTER

Drawing and Painting: In the spring when the trees are budding and the first flowers and buds are appearing on the bushes, the teacher has the children draw from nature.

The children learn to show a simple movement of the human body by changing the position of the arms and legs ("The children are doing exercises," "The puppet is dancing").

They are able to depict simple spring scenes: a tree in blossom, bushes, trees sprouting leaves, a meadow covered with flowers, a ship or boat in the river, etc.; to do a drawing using the theme of a fairy tale, song, or poem (fairy tales such as "The Fox, the Hare, and the Rooster," and "The Red Hat"; poems about spring, etc.).

The children develop skill in conveying the spatial relations between objects, arranging along a single strip on the bottom of the sheet the objects which are on the ground, and at the top of the sheet placing those which are in the air and way up in the sky.

The children make designs on a circle or polygon, alternating in a regular fashion branches, flowers, leaves, and berries, which they represent through spots, wavy lines, etc.

Modeling: The children learn to model dishes of various shapes, using for the most part a single piece of clay. They smooth out the surface with their fingers (which are first moistened in water if the figure is to be painted over). Observations of domestic animals and birds (roosters, hens, and chickens, dogs, and puppies, etc.) will help the children to model these figures correctly.

Cutting and Pasting: [The children] further develop the ability to cut out circular shapes (tulips, chickens, etc.) from traces on rectangular pieces of paper, to cut out several identical forms simultaneously from a piece of paper that has been folded up, and to make circular designs of leaves and flowers.

Construction: [The children] build pretty structures on the basis of observations, drawings, and photographs (a school building, a subway, exhibition pavilion, etc.).

FOURTH QUARTER

In the summer the children draw, paint, model, and make cut-outs on the basis of their observations of the phenomena of nature and the events of the surrounding life, applying all the skills and abilities they have acquired during the year. They work together as a group to model things for their play, cooperate on decorative cut-out projects (large flowers, butterflies) for decorating the room, the garden and the playground on holidays; they make toys out of natural materials—fir cones, acorns, straw, corncobs (dishes, boats, dolls, animals), using paste, paints, scissors, and a hammer.

Physical Development

[*Objectives*]

To improve the children's ability to walk and run correctly:. long
pace, freely swinging arms, and coordination of leg movements;
to train the children to get more spring off the ground when
they are running

To develop better spatial orientation and the ability to follow the
teacher's commands regarding direction and speed

To develop a sense of balance in the children (while in motion and
while standing still)

To further their skill in jumping: pushing off the floor or ground
energetically and swinging the arms freely and naturally;
landing lightly, with the legs bent at the knees

To teach the children to exert force when they are throwing for distance or throwing at a target, and to teach them how to throw
little balls and sandbags

To strengthen the habit of alternating the right and left feet while
climbing and of coordinating arm and leg movements. To teach
the children to arrange themselves into formations quickly and
in an orderly fashion on a command from the teacher

To train the children to adopt the proper initial position for exercises and to perform the exercises with precision. To develop
proper posture

FIRST QUARTER

Walking, Running, Exercises for Balance: Walking and running, one
behind the other, singly and in pairs, speeding up or slowing down on a
command from the teacher (tambourine, musical accompaniment), and
making turns at a signal from the teacher; walking along a board or a
bench (width 15–20 centimeters, height 25–30 centimeters), forward and
sideways.

Jumping: Leaping up for an object suspended 5 or 10 centimeters
above the out-stretched arms of the child; jumping forward on both feet
(distance 3 or 4 meters); jumping down from a height (20–30
centimeters).

Throwing: Bouncing a ball on the ground (diameter 10–15 centimeters), throwing a ball and catching it with both hands four or five
times in a row without dropping it.

Climbing: Climbing up an inclined ladder or board, climbing through a hoop, and climbing under a bar (height 40–50 centimeters).

SECOND QUARTER

Walking, Running, Exercises for Balance: Walking and running off in all directions, spreading out over the whole area of the room or playground without bumping into each other; walking and running in a column between objects which have been strewn about without touching any of them. Walking and running in a circle, holding hands or holding on to a cord; walking on tiptoe. Walking and running along an inclined board (width 15–20 centimeters, height 25–30 centimeters).

Jumping: Jumping forward (2 or 3 meters); on two feet with an object grasped between the knees; hopping from one foot to the other, in place, and moving forward; doing a standing broad jump (40–50 centimeters).

Throwing: Throwing a ball back and forth to each other (distance 1½ meters). Tossing rings on a pole, quoits (distance 1½ meters).

Climbing: Climbing to the edge of a gymnastics apparatus and climbing down gracefully without releasing one's grip on the rungs (height 2 meters).

THIRD QUARTER

Walking, Running, Exercises for Balance: Rolling a hoop in a straight line, racing (up to 12 or 13 meters), walking along a rope balancing a sandbag on the head.

Jumping: Doing a running high jump (15–20 centimeters), doing a running broad jump (30–40 centimeters).

Throwing: Throwing a ball or bag at a vertical or horizontal target, from a distance of 1½ meters, left-handed, and 2 meters, right-handed; throwing a ball over a net with two hands and catching it.

Climbing: Crawling on all fours along a bench, inclined ladder, or board; climbing over a bench, log, inclined ladder, or board.

FOURTH QUARTER

Walking, Running, Exercises for Balance: Running under a jump rope, running away from someone (playing tag), catching a person running away, standing on one foot, walking and running along a horizontal or inclined log.

Jumping: Doing a running high jump (20–25 centimeters), doing a running broad jump (50–60 centimeters), skipping rope (individually and with a longer rope held by two other children).

Throwing: Throwing balls (diameter 6–8 centimeters), sandbags, fir cones, and pebbles for distance, right-handed and left-handed; throwing a ball (diameter 20–25 centimeters) for distance from behind the head, using both hands. Throwing a ball at a ring attached at a height of 1½–2 meters above the ground.

Exercises for the Development of Specific Groups of Muscles

Exercises for the Shoulder Muscles   Raise the arms up, with or without objects (flags, poles, ropes, hoops, balls). Perform exercises standing up, with the feet parallel, sitting on a chair, on a bench, or on the floor. Lift a pole up and lower it onto the shoulders. Swing the arms forward and back, lifting them higher at each swing, and clapping hands in front and in back.

With the arms in a position in front of the chest, alternately extend them to the side and bend them; rotate the arms both together and in turn, with the arms extended straight out.

Exercises for the Leg Muscles   Squat down gripping the back of a chair (grasping the back with the arms kept straight and the knees widely separated) and squat down without supporting with the arms. Perform squatting exercises with hoops, poles, ropes, and flags. Do two or three knee bends, squatting down lower at each turn; extend each leg in turn forward and to the side. Lift the right and left foot alternately, while bending at the knees, and touch the knees, grasp them, or touch them with a rope, pole, or hoop. Raise up on tiptoe. Make right and left turns in place, following a cord laid on the ground.

Exercises for the Muscles of the Torso   Make right and left turns with the feet together, sitting on the floor with the knees hunched up and with a hoop, a ball, or a pole across the shoulders or under the arms. Bend forward, down, and to the side from an upright position and with the legs as far apart as the shoulders (the "woodcutter" or "pump" exercise); touch the tips of the feet, lay an object down in front of one and on the side, and pick it up again. Lift one's legs straight up from a sitting position (leaning backward on the hands) and then, while prone, lower them again. Lift the head and shoulders off the floor while lying on the stomach, keeping the legs straight and extending the arms to the side (the "airplane").

Drills and Formations

Form single and double columns, and form a single column to reform into several columns (three or four). Make right and left turns following instructions given in terms of some object ("Turn to the right toward the window").

Active Games

"The Agile Mouse," "Do the Following Figure," "The Carp and the Pike," "Don't Be Left on the Floor," "Who Will Reach His Flag First," "First One to His Place," "Take the Flag," "Who Jumps Best," "Who Reaches the Flag First" (involves climbing under objects), "The Bear and the Bees," "Hunters and Hares," "Throw at the Flag," "Throw into the Hoop," "Hit the Ball," and various types of individual ball games.

Sports

Sleigh Riding Sleigh ride down a hill alone, and two at a time; pull each other along. Slide along icy paths.

Skiing Walk on skis, alternately sliding on the left and right ski. Making right and left turns in place. Climb up a hill and ski down the hill bending slightly at the knees. Get the skis [without help] and put them back in the right place, put on and take off skis [without help]; carry skis under the arms.

Cycling Ride a two-wheeled bicycle in a straight line, with the assistance of an adult and alone. Make left and right turns with an adult's help.

Bathing (preparation for swimming) Play and splash around in a shallow stream, lake, or pool. Float on the stomach and take breaths. Learn to kick, sitting in a shallow spot and lying flat, supported by the hands.

Musical Training

Objectives

To arouse interest in music and to instill a love for music in the children; to expand their musical impressions and, through music, to foster a love for their native land and for their native district

To encourage the practice of listening to music in a group and to develop a memory for music by having the children try to rec-

ognize songs and musical compositions from their introduc-
tions or melodies; to teach the children to distinguish between
dances, lullabies, and marches

To work toward expressive individual and group performances of
songs, dances, and musical games; to strengthen further the
habit of good posture while singing (sitting and standing), to
preserve the children's voices in musical games and dances by
limiting the range of pitch in the selection of songs; to further
their singing skills by systematically repeating the repertory
built up by the children in the preceding groups

To develop the children's ability to carry a tune by stressing correct
pitch, to develop in the children a sense of rhythm by changing
tempos and emphasizing the beat, to stimulate their desire to be
independent and not imitate each other when portraying the
characters in musical games

Singing   It is very important to train the children to sing with expression: to sing smoothly and lightly in a natural voice without
straining, to take breaths between musical phrases; to pronounce the
words correctly and distinctly; to begin and end a song all together, to
stay on pitch, and to observe the appropriate dynamics. To sing at different tempos, with the teacher but without the accompaniment of a musical instrument, and independently with the accompaniment of a musical
instrument.

Musical-Rhythmic Movements   The children should learn to pick up
less obvious contrasts in the character of the music, in the dynamics
(loud, moderately loud, soft, louder, softer) and to reflect this ability by
making corresponding changes in their movements. They should go from
a deliberate to a fast or slow tempo, they should convey the beat and
rhythm by clapping their hands and be able to change their movements
appropriately in musical pieces involving two or three different forms.

The children learn to do the following types of movements in time to
the music: walk lightly and gracefully, run rapidly lifting the legs way up,
hop from one foot to the other, perform various types of movements with
objects and without, spring up on their legs, portray various types of
characters, form a circle without outside assistance and maintain the distance between pairs, contract and expand the circle, break up pairs by
going in opposite directions, and then come back together again.

They should also learn the following routine dance steps: extending the
legs forward alternately; stepping in place on the balls of the feet,
bending slightly at the knees; raising and lowering the arms gracefully,
forward and to the side; spinning around in pairs; and circling around a

partner, back to back. The children are taught dances comprised of these elements.

Music for Listening: "Field March," music by D. Kabalevsky; "Lullaby," music by N. Rimsky-Korsakov; "The Cuckoo," music by M. Krasev.

Singing: "Chiki-chiki, Chikalochki," "Bai, Kachi, Kachi," Russian folk lullabies; "Holiday Song," music by M. Jordansky; "Our Guests Have Arrived," music by A. Alexandrov.

Games to Songs and Instrumental Music: "The Raven," Russian folk song; "Tambourine Game," music by M. Krasev; "The Cat and the Mice," music by T. Lomova.

Dances and Exercises: "The Invitation," Ukranian folk song; "Riders and Bridles," music by V. Vitlin.

Music for Listening: "Grandfather's Story," music by N. Lubarsky; "The Goslings," German folk song; "The Clowns," music by D. Kabalevsky.

Singing: "The Blue Sleighs," music by M. Jordansky; "Grandfather Frost," music by V. Vitlin; "Song of the New Year's Tree," music by E. Tilicheeva.

Games to Songs and Instrumental Music: "Vas'ka the Cat," music by G. Lobachev; "Lovishki," music by I. Gaidn.

Dances and Exercises: "Don't Be Late," music by M. Raukhverger; "Dance of the Hare Musicians," music by A. Zhilinsky; "Pass the Scarf," music by T. Lomova.

Music for Listening: "Song of Lenin," music by M. Krasev; "The Bold Horseman," music by R. Schumann; "The Wolf and the Hares," music by E. Tilicheeva; "Evening Song," music by V. Gerchik; "The Butterfly," music by S. Maikapar.

Singing: "The Spring-fly," music by A. Filippenko; "My Flag," music by V. Gerchik; "The Kindergarten," music by A. Filippenko; "Geese and Goslings," music by A. Alexandrov.

Games to Songs and Instrumental Music: "Be Agile," music by N. Ladykhin; "Pilots, Watch the Weather," music by M. Raukhverger; "Game of the Bells," music by Y. Rozhavskaya; "Scarf Game," Ukranian folk tune.

Dances and Exercises: "Ukranian Dance," Ukranian folk tune; "Rattles," music by T. Bil'koreyskaya; "Circle Dance," Latvian folk tune.

FOURTH QUARTER

Music for Listening: "The Fish," music by M. Krasev; "The Young Shepherd," music by S. Maikapar; "Three Sons," Czech folk song.

Singing: "Butterflies," music by M. Krasev; "Let's Go to the Raspberry Garden," "Song of the Frogs and the Mosquito," music by A. Filippenko.

Games to Songs and Instrumental Music: "Circle Dance in the Woods," music by M. Jordansky.

HOLIDAYS AND CELEBRATIONS

Children in the older group are given greater opportunities for active participation in the preparations for the national holidays: The Great October Socialist Revolution, the First of May, and International Women's Day (the Eighth of March), as well as taking part in the preparations for the New Year's celebration.

The children prepare gifts and decorations for the rooms and the playground and draw up invitations for the party.

It is essential to provide for the active participation of every child in the morning party by arranging for various types of individual and group performances. The preparations for these performances need not be long or burdensome to the children.

The teachers take note of the children's birthdays and from time to time arrange parties for the children involving shows, dramatizations of fairy tales, "circus games," concerts, and Punch and Judy shows where the puppet does tricks and proposes riddles.

VII

The School
Preparatory Group

SEVENTH YEAR OF
THE CHILD'S LIFE

EDUCATIONAL OBJECTIVES

The educational and instructional work for this group is directed at the all-around development of the children. Its content is to a considerable degree determined by objectives related to preparing the children for school. It is essential to strengthen the health of the children in every way possible; to take excellent care of their hearing, sight, and voices; and to reinforce good health habits, cleanliness, and courtesy. The teacher should strive to broaden the child's conceptions of the life of society and his conceptions of nature and to help to orient the child in every respect. It is extremely important to develop phonemic discrimination in hearing and the ability to analyze visual and auditory stimuli; to develop inquisitiveness and the powers of observation and memory—all of these attributes are essential in learning how to read and write. Much attention must be devoted to developing moral behavior, organization, a collective spirit, respect for elders, and concern for younger children. It is important to develop in the children the ability and desire to join together and cooperate in activities. Through the colorful social events which are within the range of understanding of the children, the teacher must strive to develop in them a love for their native district and their native land and friendly feelings for people of other nationalities. Love for nature and appreciation of art must also be fostered.

CHARACTERISTICS OF CHILDREN
AT THIS AGE

Intensive physical development continues to take place in children in their seventh year, and their movements become more precise and better coordinated. Along with the basic physical skills, more delicate finger and hand movements are developed. The general efficiency and stability of the nervous system gradually increase. The role of speech in the psychological processes of the child also increases, and for this reason the child's awareness of his conduct and his will power must be intensively developed.

The child becomes stronger in the course of his seventh year, and more able to withstand regular and relatively long physical and mental exertions. The relations between adults and children become more complex and more diverse. The child participates with adults in common activities and sometimes helps out the adults. Although he is not in constant need of adult assistance, the child nevertheless requires constant personal contact with adults in order to increase his knowledge and to receive instructions and advice concerning the goals and the planning of his activities and the techniques necessary to perform specific actions. This need for personal contact arises not only in connection with immediate tangible problems and concerns but also independently.

The child can converse about what he has found out from past experiences and what has interested him in past events.

The role of the children's collective in forming each child's personality becomes even more crucial. More stable and more complex relationships grow up among the children. The ability to cooperate and to organize things without outside assistance increases; rudimentary collective opinions emerge, leading to a system whereby very elementary rules of procedure are announced by the children themselves to every participant in a common undertaking (in play, activities, and work).

Along with further development of creative role-playing and construction games, considerable attention is given to active games involving rules and to educational games. Simple forms of work assume greater and greater significance in the lives of the children. The children develop a conscientious, serious attitude toward activities and toward elementary study habits.

The child's perceptiveness and powers of observation are exploited fully—he applies them to a specific problem and systematically familiarizes himself with a particular object or illustration. The creativity and imagination of the children are further developed, and at this age they become more directed.

The child's memory develops, and one can detect attempts on his part to group material by sense associations and to utilize independently simple memorization techniques (repetition, etc.).

Considerable changes occur in the thought and speech of the child. His vocabulary expands, the structure of his sentences improves, and his ability to relate stories in a connected way and without skipping over details increases.

The child begins to make more complex generalizations. He develops the ability to compare concrete objects and groups of objects and even to compare elementary concepts. It is very important to arrange the instructional process in such a way that the aggregate of these concepts will lead the child to a correct and materialistic understanding of surrounding realities.

At the older preschool age, will power and the emotional characteristics of personality undergo intensive development. Interest increases in adult life, as does the urge to participate in work activities. Children at this age are capable of understanding that the activities of the people around them are directed at satisfying not only personal needs but also the needs of others. As a result, the children acquire the ability to judge not only their own acts but those of others, and to regulate their own conduct not merely by submitting to external demands, but also by relating it to the moral concepts and feelings rapidly developing within them.

ORGANIZATION OF THE LIFE OF THE GROUP AND EDUCATION OF THE CHILDREN

The life of the group is organized in such a way as to insure a diversity of activities for the children. The daily schedule provides for morning exercises, activities, play and work, an extended period outside, meals, and an afternoon nap. Eating, sleeping, dressing, and washing proceed at a faster rate in this group and therefore take up less time. In performing these routine procedures, the children do not require constant assistance. The teacher trusts them to do on their own what is required of them. The teacher should develop in the children a need to be occupied with· something constantly and should train them to select things which they enjoy doing.

The role of activities increases, both in the realization of the educational instructional aspect of the program and in the mental and moral development of the children. The nature of the activities must contribute to the development and enrichment of all the various activities of the children: play, work, and artistic endeavors. The children enjoy listening to readings, music, and songs. Work in the nature of self-service, and also work benefiting the group as a whole, plays a more and more central role in the lives of the children.

In the afternoon the teacher satisfies the needs of the children for repeated listening to literary and musical works, trains them to apply the skills and habits they have acquired in activity periods to independent creative activity of all kinds, and adds depth and breadth to the interests of the children.

In the summer period, the daily schedule is changed. The second activity period is dropped, and the time spent working in the flower and vegetable gardens is increased. The entire life of the group is transferred into the open air.

Conditioning

The objective is to reinforce habits and practices acquired in the previous groups.

Play, activities, and the afternoon nap are all conducted with the vents open, and in summer with the windows open or out in the open air.

In very cold weather, the vents are opened periodically, without however ever permitting the air temperature in the room to drop by more than one or two degrees. The children sleep on the verandas with the windows open.

The outdoor recreation period is held every day regardless of the weather and lasts on the average of three to four hours (the only exceptions to this occur in freezing and rainy weather). The teacher makes sure that all the children participate in various games, sports, and collective work.

Sponging of the legs should begin at a temperature of $+26°$ C., with the temperature being lowered by one degree every three or four days until it reaches $+16°$ C.

Wet rubs should begin with the temperature at $+28°$ C., decreasing it by one degree every two or three days until it reaches $+16°$. Sponging the body begins with the water temperature at $+30°$ C., decreasing it every three or four days by one degree until it reaches $+18°$ or $+17°$ in the summer, and $+24°$ in the other seasons.

Bathing in a river, lake, or sea should begin when the water temperature is not below $+22°$ C. and the temperature of the air is not below $+24°$; bathing should commence only after the children have been systematically conditioned by spongings. The children should bathe once a day. They go into the water in small groups and stay in for from two to four up to eight or ten minutes. After bathing, the children are quickly and thoroughly dried. In cool weather, spongings or wet rubs replace bathing.

Sun baths are taken when prescribed by the doctor, and are taken under his supervision.

Morning Exercises

Morning exercises are conducted every day, lasting for eight to ten minutes. The morning gymnastic routines consist of four or five exercises for various groups of muscles. Each of the exercises is repeated six or eight times. A series of exercises is performed involving various objects (hoops, flags, poles). On warm days the morning exercises are conducted on the playground.

Training in Interpersonal Relations

The sphere of personal contacts of a 6-year-old child with other people expands. The children find themselves more frequently in public places and they converse with a larger circle of people; therefore, it is imperative that feelings of respect and friendliness toward people be developed and that courteous habits be reinforced. The children should greet people, speak to them politely, ask questions courteously and say "goodbye" to them.

The children should know that in greeting someone they should not extend their hands: this may only be done when the adult himself offers his hand. The teacher instructs the children to listen attentively to what an adult is saying; when answering him, to look him in the face; to carry out quickly and willingly requests or demands, to yield the right of way to an adult, and to stoop and pick things up for adults. She trains the children to be concerned for the welfare of other people, develops in the children the ability to take into consideration the opinions of others when judging their own acts, and strives to give them a concept of good and bad (to speak the truth is good, to be rude or to offend the younger children is bad, etc.).

Training in Self-sufficiency, Hygiene, Cleanliness, and Courtesy

The children are trained to wash and dry themselves quickly and thoroughly at the proper times and whenever the need arises; to use a handkerchief, to make sure a clean one is available, to wipe their mouths off in the morning and after dinner, and to clean their teeth; to dress and undress quickly; to keep their clothing and footwear clean and tidy, and to notice whenever anything is out of order in their clothing—to sew on a button, clean their clothes or shoes; to help each other and the younger children in dressing and undressing.

The children should always observe proper table manners wherever they may be: they should drink and swallow food quietly; use their spoons, knives, and forks in the correct manner; eat quickly and without becoming distracted; and drink only sterilized water in a clean glass.

The children should take an active interest in keeping the common room and the playground clean and orderly.

Broadening Orientation to the Environment: Speech Development

The children show interest in events in the surrounding life and in nature; together with adults they experience the events of social significance which are most closely related to their lives, and they observe and experience the seasonal changes in nature. Intellectual and esthetic inquiries on the part of the children increase in quantity and scope. The teacher encourages and guides the interests of the children, their curiosity, and their feelings of excitement; she utilizes the impressions received by the children from their environment to add breadth and depth to their perspective, to develop their powers of thought and speech, to instill in them a desire for work, and to further develop the richness and meaningfulness of their play activities.

In order to develop friendly feelings in the children toward the other nationalities of the Soviet Union, it is very important to exploit fully significant social events throughout the year, national holidays, encounters and correspondence with other people, the singing of the songs of other nationalities, and the viewing of illustrations.

Excursions and conversations with the children contribute to broadening and making more secure the children's orientation in the building and on the premises of the kindergarten and in the streets in the area surrounding the kindergarten. Temporal orientation improves. The children learn to name all the hours of the day, the days of the week, and the seasons of the year. The children learn to name household objects and to use them correctly. During the outdoor recreation period the teachers expand the children's ideas of nature, develop an interest in and love for nature, and implant a desire in the children to cultivate and take care of plants and to look after useful animals. The children develop the ability to relate changes in weather conditions to the lives of plants and animals and to record their observations on a nature calendar.

Year round weather observations are conducted—sunny; overcast; clouds; storm clouds up in the sky; wind (light, strong, faint breeze); rain (fine, heavy, downpour); snowfall (isolated snowflakes, fine snow, large snowflakes); snow storm; cold; freezing; thawing; hot; thunder; rainbow; hail; etc. The child's vocabulary correspondingly expands. His attention is drawn to seasonal changes in plant and animal life and to meteorological events and shifts in the weather.

Fall   In the fall the children observe changes in the color of the leaves on the trees and on the bushes; they watch the leaves fall to the ground, collect seeds and fruit to feed the birds in the winter, watch the birds migrate, and observe the days grow shorter. The children help transplant plants from the flowerbed to the nature corner.

Winter   In the winter the children note the appearance of the trees in various kinds of weather, observe the habits of the winter birds, etc. On the playground the children set up a feeding station for the birds and then feed them regularly.

Spring   In the spring the children observe changes in the snow (crumbly, dirty), the appearance of streams, melting icicles, the budding of the trees, the appearance of leaves, the arrival of the birds, and the lengthening of the day; they help to hang out wooden boxes for the starlings, watch how the birds make their homes in them, and watch the baby birds fly out. The children actively participate in making flower borders, in planting seeds, and in transplanting flower and vegetable seedlings.

Summer   In the summer the children observe the changes in the flowers covering the meadows and the flowers coming up in the flower garden; they watch the vegetables ripen in the vegetable garden and watch for the appearance of mushrooms and berries in the woods. The teacher develops in the children an attitude of care for trees and birds and the ability to appreciate the beauty of nature.

Throughout the year the teacher works to develop the children's ability to communicate: she encourages meaningful conversations and stories about what the children have seen and heard. She trains them to talk slowly and expressively and to relate events in order. She helps them to find vital words; checks their grammar and pronunciation; encourages and develops a love for poetry, short stories, and fairy tales, arouses an interest in books and the desire to discover what is written in them and to discuss what has been read. She stimulates the children's interest in and love for songs and music; she develops a feeling for the precise, expressive word; in talking with the children, she herself uses appropriate epithets, sayings, and proverbs.

WORK

The work activities of the children develop along the lines of broader and more involved work obligations and more complex forms of organizing the work, as well as more intense feelings of responsibility for the performance of chores and errands. The teacher reinforces the interest and enjoyment of the children in all forms of work, teaches them to do work on their own initiative and not merely at the request of the teacher, and to take good care of materials and tools. She develops in the children the ability to judge the quality of their own work and that of the other children. The teacher should develop the children's ability to agree among themselves when beginning a cooperative job; to distribute the various tasks among themselves; and to work together harmoniously, giving each other needed assistance. She should broaden the children's perspective on certain types of routine work and plant and animal care; she should develop a respect for the work of all the kindergarten personnel and a desire to be of assistance to them. The children's work should be purposeful, and they should derive happiness and satisfaction from it.

The work activities in the children occur at various times during the day. In the morning (before the activity period) children on duty do dining room work, take care of the plants and animals in the nature corner, and prepare materials for the activities. Children work in the vegetable and flower gardens mainly in the morning and evening. In cases where it is necessary to demonstrate work techniques to all of the children (planting, grafting, and working with tools), it is best to call the whole group together. For routine everyday jobs, the children work in small groups.

Routine Housework

The children participate in cleaning up the common room daily; with damp cloths they wipe off the chairs, the window sills, and the building materials. They wash off toys and clean and press dolls' clothing, ribbons, collars and socks. This type of work is organized at the end of the week, in the afternoon. Throughout the year the children work on the playground, sweep and decorate it, brush away the snow, and rake off the leaves.

Cultivation of the Plants and Care of the Animals

The children should be able to determine by themselves when the plants in the nature corner need watering, should watch to make sure the plants in the room are kept clean, and should sprinkle them whenever necessary.

In the fall the children prepare soil and sand for the nature corner and collect seeds from the plants.

In the winter they feed the winter birds, look after the fish and other creatures in the aquarium, keep the animals' cages clean (they clean out the cages, sprinkle sand, and give the animals food and water), and under the teacher's supervision change the water in the aquarium.

In the spring the children break off dry leaves, cultivate the ground, and fertilize and water the seedlings on instructions from the teacher.

In the summer they water, cultivate, weed, fertilize, and make little splints to which certain of the plants are tied (peas, lima beans). In their own little plot, as well as in the garden adjoining the *kolkhoz* or *sovkhoz* (state farm), the children can take an active role in the harvesting.

Under the teacher's supervision the children grow plants by cutting off shoots and planting them (both for school and to give as gifts to their parents).

Work of the Children on Duty

The increasing physical strength and the accumulated experiences of the children make it feasible to increase the complexity of the chores for which the children on duty are responsible and, at the same time, to raise the standard of quality demanded in their performance. The children on duty should promptly and quickly distribute materials and equipment for the activities and should collect them again at the proper time. The children on duty in the dining room should set the table, serve the second and third courses at dinner, clear the dishes from the table, sweep the floor, and water the plants; they are also responsible for noting down the weather conditions on the calendar. It is important to promote courtesy toward others and a concern for the welfare of others. The children should also be trained to be graceful and agile, to handle objects skillfully, and to work at a sufficiently rapid pace. The children perform various duties in groups of two or three; in addition, longer individual work assignments (lasting for one to two weeks) are introduced into the work schedule, for example: taking care of a particular plant or animal and maintaining order in the cupboard containing the books and educational games. Chores which are assigned for relatively long periods contribute to the development of a sense of responsibility.

Handicraft

The children work with wood (they nail, saw, paint) and make various objects and toys. The children learn to use a hammer, scissors, tongs, penknives, and pliers.

Woodworking is done on the playground in the spring and summer, with small groups of children working together.

The children learn to make useful things out of paper, cardboard, cloth, and wood (pots for plants, waste paper baskets, book bags, feeding stations for the birds, and little shelves); to make simple toys (airplanes, toy furniture); and to sew doll clothing and little seed bags.

Working with paper and cardboard involves folding, pasting, stitching, cutting with scissors, and cutting things out according to a pattern. Under the teacher's supervision the children make toys and equipment and repair toys and books. They learn to thread needles, tie knots, and sew on buttons and tabs.

ACTIVITIES

For the school preparatory group there are two activity periods, lasting 25 to 30 minutes.

In the activities, efforts are continued in the direction of broadening the children's conceptions of the environment, cultivating an interest in work, and engendering a respect for working people. The children are taught to observe, to compare, to make simple deductions, to express their thoughts concisely, and to make generalizations; the role of language in the instruction of the children continually increases. The children become better oriented spatially, and their visual and auditory powers increase. The work demands made upon the children increase, and independence and creative initiative are encouraged. The children develop the ability to correct and assist each other, to answer questions put by the teacher to the whole group, to use both long- and short-form answers, to follow a topic of conversation, to express their opinions on a subject, and to ask pertinent questions themselves. In all the activities the teacher is careful to stress correct and expressive speech.

Familiarization with the Environment

The teacher should strive to develop in the children a feeling of attachment for their native district, to broaden their ideas of their native land and of the working people, and to stimulate their curiosity. Through observations, discussions and stories, the children should be trained to use precise terminology for objects and to bring into active use words designating general concepts; the vocabulary of the children should be expanded as they are taught to use the correct terms for the professions and occupations of people, for animals, and for objects and their properties.

FIRST QUARTER

School: All children enter school at the age of 7 to study and learn. Six-year-old children are preparing for school. School children study diligently and work hard. The nearest school is located on . . . (the children should know the address).

Native City, Settlement, Town, or Village: The children should become familiar with the work of the people in the area surrounding the kindergarten (construction sites, factories, stores, schools, libraries, etc.).

The children should learn thoroughly the rules regarding walking along the street: to walk calmly on the sidewalk, not to play on the pavement, to cross the street with adults at fixed locations, and to know the traffic light signals.

Moscow: the Capital of the Soviet Union: Our government does its work in Moscow, in the Kremlin; it concerns itself with the welfare of all the people in the Soviet Union. V. I. Lenin lived and worked in Moscow.

The largest and most beautiful square in Moscow is Red Square.

The Seventh of November: In Red Square, on the holiday celebrating the Great October Socialist Revolution, there are worker demonstrations and a parade by the Soviet Army. Guests from our constituent republics and from other countries arrive for the holiday.

The Labor of the Kolkhoz Workers: In the fall the *kolkhoz* workers harvest wheat, rye, corn, potatoes, sugarbeets, and carrots in the fields; they pick the fruit in the gardens and pluck off the grapes. The harvest from the *kolkhozes* and *sovkhozes* (which differ in many respects from the *kolkhozes* or collective farms) is transported on trains by the railroad workers, on ships by the sailors, and on planes by pilots.

Bread, fruit, and vegetables are bought in stores and in stalls.

Nature, in the Fall: The changes in the plant and animal life are related to the approach of cold weather. The flowers have withered, the grass has turned yellow, and the leaves on the trees have turned yellow and are falling off.

The beetles, butterflies, and frogs have disappeared. The birds (rooks, starlings) are gathering into flocks and flying away to warmer climates.

The children should be able to distinguish and describe the characteristic features of familiar plants and to differentiate two or three types of trees by their leaves and fruits; for example, oaks, spruces, pines, maples, and ash trees.

SECOND QUARTER

The Preparation of Food: Various types of groceries are needed for the preparation of food: meat, fish, groats, vegetables, milk, sour cream, and butter. Groceries are kept in the refrigerator.

Various types of equipment and machines are helpful in preparing tasty meals quickly (meat grinders, vegetable cutters, potato peelers).

What People Ride On: Our country is large. People ride on trains, in airplanes, and on ships; they transport freight to cities, to *kolkhozes*, and to construction sites. Aviators, mechanics, and radio operators work on planes; engineers, machinists, and conductors work on trains; captains, sailors, and radio operators work on ships.

The Library: In the library there are many books. The librarian tries to see that the readers obtain interesting books and she signs books out to them to take home. Books are kept on shelves.

The children become accustomed to taking books out of a library which is organized and set up within the group; an interest in books and an attitude of care toward books are developed.

International Woman's Day, the Eighth of March: This day is a holiday for all working women. The children prepare presents for their mothers, teachers, relatives, and close friends.

Clothing: Clothing is made by tailors and dressmakers, in workshops and in factories. The *kolkhoz* workers (Uzbeks, Kazakhi, and other nationalities) raise many sheep. The sheep are shorn. The wool is transported to the factories. From wool, yarn is made; from yarn, mittens, socks, jackets, scarves, and other articles of clothing are made.

Nature, in the Winter: In the winter the sun sets early—the day is short and the night is long. In the sky, the stars and moon appear early. There are snowfalls, snow storms, and thaws. In freezing weather the snow is dry and it crumbles and crunches under foot, while in thaws the snow is wet and sticks. It is cold for the birds and they fly up to people's houses. People make feeding stations and feed the birds (the children should observe the habits of the birds which fly up to the feeding stations). In the winter there are no leaves on the branches of the trees, but there are seed pods.

The children learn to recognize and to name correctly the four or five types of birds most frequently encountered in the area (sparrows, crows, jackdaws, rooks, bluebirds).

The children should be able to recognize a few types of trees by the bark, by the branches, and by the shapes of the crowns of the trees. They should notice the appearance of trees in different kinds of weather: in a freezing spell, during a snowfall, and when there is a thaw. They should know the various parts of the plants in the rooms and be able to name their color and shape.

THIRD QUARTER

The Twenty-second of April, Lenin's Birthday: The children are read poems about V. I. Lenin and are told stories about selected events in his life. The children bring flowers to the monument of V. I. Lenin and make albums of illustrations of his life. Excursions are arranged to places connected with the life of Vladimir Ilyich.

The First of May, the Holiday of Workers All over the World: On May 1, in Red Square in Moscow, there are worker demonstrations and a parade by the Soviet army.

The Nationalities in Our Country: In our country live Russians, Ukranians, Belorussians, Uzbeks, and people of other nationalities. All work together as friends, help each other, and love their native land.

Friendly attitudes and feelings toward other nationalities are developed in the children.

Construction: Workers build apartment houses, kindergartens, schools, etc. Plumbers lay water pipes and install heating in the buildings, and electricians install the electrical wiring. Cranes, power shovels, etc. facilitate the work of these laborers.

Nature, in the Spring: Warm weather sets in, the snow melts and patches of ground appear, streams begin to flow, and in the rivers ice drifts and floods occur. On the trees the buds swell and burst open, and downy leaves and blossoms appear. The rooks, starlings and swallows fly back from warmer countries. The birds must be cared for. Wooden boxes for the starlings are hung up in gardens and on the boulevards. Trees and bushes are planted in gardens and along the streets, and they are carefully attended to insure that they grow well: little trenches are dug around them and they are watered, lime is sprinkled on them, and harmful insects are destroyed.

The workers on the *kolkhoz* prepare the fields for sowing (plow, fertilize) and take care of the area which has already been sown (weed, cultivate, water).

The children learn to plant seeds and to transplant seedlings in the flowerbeds and in the vegetable garden.

FOURTH QUARTER

Nature, in the Summer: The sun shines brightly. It is hot and the day is long. There are thunder storms (there is lightning and thunder, and rain and hail fall). After the rain, when the sun is shining, a rainbow appears (the children should know the colors of the rainbow).

The children should be able to distinguish a few types of trees by their fruits and their leaves (acorns, cones, pappi), for example, oaks, spruces, pines, maples, ash trees; they should also be able to distinguish trees by their bark and the arrangement of their branches. The trees blossom, and in place of flowers seed pods and fruits appear. In the summer mushrooms and berries are gathered in the woods.

The children should be able to recognize and name correctly the most common butterflies—cabbage, lemon-tree, and nettle butterflies, etc., and such beetles as the May beetle, dung beetle and carabus.

Butterflies lay eggs (larvae) on plants, and moths emerge and begin to eat the leaves. The larvae and the moths should be destroyed.

The children should be familiar with lizards, turtles and frogs, what they look like and what they eat. They should understand the relationship between the length of an animal's legs and the speed at which it moves; they should know that fish live in rivers, lakes, and ponds.

Occupations: During the summer the children develop fuller conceptions of the work of the people on the *kolkhozes* and of that of the construction workers. The children learn that in the fields are grown rye, wheat, oats and corn, and on the meadows, grass. At haying time the *kolkhoz* workers gather the grass from the meadows; they cut it with scythes, dry it, and rake it into stacks. The hay is stored until winter when it will be used to feed the animals.

The children learn that the crop (vegetables and grains) depends on the care given to the plants (if the ground is cultivated, the soil is fertilized, and the weeds pulled out, there will be a good crop).

On the *kolkhoz* cows, pigs, sheep, and domestic fowl are raised; cow shelters, stables, and pig sties are built for the animals. Grooms, milkmaids, and other special workers look after the domestic animals. New houses, clubs, and kindergartens are being built in the towns.

The Pioneers: The children learn of the life of the pioneers from books and from stories related by the teacher. The pioneers try to study well, work hard, assist younger children, and give help to older people. In the summer the pioneers vacation and work in camps and help with the work of the *kolkhoz.*

Domestic and Wild Animals: It is extremely important to reinforce and expand throughout the year all the knowledge of wild and domestic animals which the children have thus far accumulated. The children should know the characteristic features in the appearance of different animals, as well as their habits.

The children learn and name from memory the characteristic features of wild animals (squirrels, bears, foxes, wolves, hares, tigers, lions, elephants, and monkeys); they know their habitats and their chief habits.

Native Language

In the activity periods devoted to the native language, the child's vocabulary is increased and put to more active use; precision of speech is developed, along with a feeling for words and a sensitivity of shades of meaning; the children are trained to sense and comprehend the meaning and beauty in figures of speech and images (in riddles, rhymes, and fairy tales). There is systematic instruction in connected, grammatically correct, and expressive speech. Throughout the year the sound aspect of the child's speech is developed: distinct pronunciation and expressive intonation. A new objective is set—the development of phonemic discrimination and the phonological analysis of speech. The children are trained to listen to answers attentively, to ask questions themselves, to notice mistakes, and to correct and supplement the answers of others.

FIRST QUARTER

In discussions and stories about things observed or heard (for instance, about the occupations of the *kolkhoz* workers or about natural phenomena in the fall), the child's vocabulary is brought into active use; he is trained to use the precise terms for objects, their parts and their properties, and for actions. In stories, where and when the described events occurred should be clearly expressed.

The children learn to relate the episodes or events in a literary text (a fairy tale or short story) in the correct order, without omissions or repetitions, to break up the stories into various parts, and to dramatize fairy tales.

Preparation for Reading and Writing: To teach the children to compose sentences of two or three words and then to divide them into separate words, to indicate the order of the words in a sentence, to distinguish the syllables and sounds in words, to join sounds into syllables and syllables into words; to become familiar with the sounds and letters а, у, о, ы [the four most frequently used hard vowels]; to teach the children to recognize these letters at the beginning of a word, in the middle, and at the end; to remember words with these sounds; and to memorize the printed forms for these letters.

SECOND QUARTER

The child should be able to tell in a sequential fashion about himself, about his games, his work, and his observations—at home and at the kindergarten; to make up short stories on the basis of what is illustrated in a picture and on the basis of a theme suggested by the teacher; and to use precise terminology and the correct grammatical forms of words.

Suggested topics: An incident which occurred on an excursion; "How we performed our work duties during dinner"; "How I made a toy automobile"; "How I bought an envelope and stamp at the post office," etc.

Preparation for Learning to Read and Write: The children should be introduced to the sounds and letters м,ш, р, с [*m, sh, r,* and *s* are the rough phonetic equivalents]; should be taught to pronounce these sounds; to distinguish them in syllables and in words; to remember words in which these sounds occur at the beginning, in the middle, and at the end; they should know how to print these letters.

The teacher familiarizes the children with the type of notebook which will be used in Grade I and explains what a page is and what a line is; she teaches the children to sit properly and to hold their pencils and notebooks correctly. The children trace lines and draw designs. The teacher gets the children ready for writing with special exercises and teaches them to draw the basic elements of the various letters with a pencil.

THIRD QUARTER

The teacher encourages the child's creativity and initiative in telling stories based on illustrations or suggested themes.

Preparation for Learning to Read and Write: The children are familiarized with the sounds and letters л, н, р, п [*l, n, r, p* are the rough phonetic equivalents]; they learn to pronounce these sounds, to distinguish them in words and syllables, and to remember words containing these particular sounds. The children's accumulated knowledge of letters and sounds is reinforced. From cardboard letters the children put together syllables and words, first using the vowel "a," then "y," and then later on the vowels "o" and "ы"; they read words and short sentences by syllables.

Drills in writing the basic elements of the letters continue.

FOURTH QUARTER

The children should be able to describe objects in a connected fashion, from observation and from memory (flowers, trees, butterflies, etc.); finding precise and expressive words by which to indicate size, shape, color, and spatial orientation; and using compound adjectives (such as dark blue, bright yellow) and adjectives in the comparative and superlative degrees.

During this period, the children's skills in retelling stories and in expressively dramatizing fairy tales is further developed.

It is essential to improve the pronunciation of the children through exercises involving tongue-twisters, rhymes, and jingles.

Artistic Literature

Artistic literature develops the esthetic appreciation of the children, deepens their sense of morality, and forms correct attitudes toward the real world.

It is extremely important to develop in the children a positive emotional response to literary works; an ear for poetry; and the ability to catch the richness of sound, the musical quality, and the flow of poetic speech. The children must develop a feeling for and an understanding of the figures of speech and the images in the language of fairy tales, stories, and poems. The children's skills in reciting stories from memory with expression and in making up stories must be reinforced; their ability to use verbal emphases, pauses, and intonations effectively and creativity must be developed through the type of instruction in expressive speech which is tied in with the dramatization games.

FIRST QUARTER

For Storytelling: "Little Sister Alenushka and Little Brother Ivanushka," traditional Russian fairy tales adapted by M. Bulatov; "The Lame Duck," traditional Russian fairy tale; "The Cuckoo," Nenetz fairy tale.

For Reading: "Tale of the Unknown Hero," S. Marshak; "The Fox's Bread," "The Porcupine," M. Prishvin; "What I Saw" (selected chapters), B. Zhitkov; "Mukha-Tsokotukha," K. Chukovsky; "Akhakhi-khophotushechka," L. Knitko; "In Lenin's Footsteps," Y. Yakovlev; "Vovka—Kind Soul," A. Barto; "A Difficult Evening," N. Artyukhova.

For Memorization: "The Flag," A. Aleksin; "Autumn! Our Poor Garden is Silhouetted . . . ," A. Tolstoy; "Help," P. Voron'ko; "November," S. Marshak; "Welcome," S. Drozhin; "Anna-Vanna, the Brigadier," L. Kvitko.

SECOND QUARTER

For Storytelling: "Tale of the Brave Hare," D. N. Mamin-Sibiryak; "Moroz Ivanovich," "The Gray Felt Coat," (traditional Russian fairy tales), V. Odoyevsky.

For Reading: "New Year's at the Falconers," A. Kononov; "What to Be?" V. Mayakovsky; "The Carp," N. Nosov; "Winter Banquet," N. Pavlova; "The Cars in Our Street," M. Ilyin and E. Segal; "Tsvetik-semi-tsvetik," V. Katayev; "Oksya, the Worker," V. Chelintseva and N. Emelyanova.

For Memorization: "The Bear in the Forest," L. Kvitko; "Happy New Year," E. Trutneva; "The New Year," A. Blok.

THIRD QUARTER

For Storytelling: "The Snow Maiden," traditional Russian fairy tale; "The Ugly Duckling," H. C. Andersen; "The Three Little Pigs," English fairy tale; "The Dove and the Grain of Wheat," [translation from Laksy (language spoken in an area of Dagestan)], N. Yusupov.

For Reading: "Tale of the Fish and the Fisherman," A. S. Pushkin; "Stories of Lenin," Bonch-Bruyevich; "Help Is on the Way," B. Zhitkov; "This Little Book of Mine is about the Oceans and a Light-house," V. Mayakovsky; "Golden Meadow," M. Prishvin; "Grandfather Mazai and the Hares," N. Nekrasov; "The Avalanche," B. Zhitkov; "The Morning Rays," K. D. Ushensky; "Two Radio Operators," S. Sakharnov; "The Airplane Flies," I. Vinokurov.

For Memorization: "Song of Spring," Y. Kolas; "On the Meadow," A. Blok; "Spring Waters," F. Tyutchev; "Colored Lights," Y. Akim.

FOURTH QUARTER

For Storytelling: "The Tsarevna-Frog," traditional Russian fairy tale; "The Twelve Months" (traditional Slovak fairy tale), S. Marshak; "The Princess and the Pea," H. C. Andersen.

For Reading: "The Hunchback Horse," P. Yershov; "The Girlfriends Go to School," L. Voronkova; "Arishka, the Coward," "Forest Huts," V. Bianki; "They Have Gone Away," A. Barto; "The Children and the Ducklings," M. Prishvin; "When This Happens," A. Rylov; "Wheels of Different Types," V. Suteyev; "Baramelei," K. Chukovsky; "Palle— Alone in the World" (translation from Danish), I. Sigsgord; "The Sparrow in the Clock," L. Tolstoy; "The House which Jack Built," S. Marshak; "Yellow, White, and Lilac," N. Pavlova; "Ravi I Shashi," S. Baruzdin.

For Memorization: "To School," Z. Alexandrov; "Nails," E. Serova; "The Well," M. Pozharova; "The Dandelion," E. Blaginina; "The Crow and the Fox," "The Dragonfly and the Ant," I. Krylov.

Computation

FIRST QUARTER

[*Objectives*]

To reinforce skill in counting up to ten: counting by ear, counting sets of identical actions, and counting by feel; counting off an indicated number of objects and actions

To teach the children to count up to ten using ordinal numbers and to differentiate between questions requiring responses in terms of ordinal numbers and those requiring responses in terms of cardinal numbers. To train children to know the number of units in numbers up to ten

Familiarization with the concept of magnitude: greater-less, smaller-larger, wider-narrower, taller-shorter, lighter-heavier, thicker-thinner

SECOND QUARTER

[*Objectives*]

To reinforce the study of the composition of digits, by breaking the digits up into units; to study the composition of digits out of two smaller digits, for the digits from one to five (working with concrete materials). Preparation for writing numbers: drawing borders consisting of points, straight and curved lines, and various angles and figures; drawing a square, a rectangle, a circle, an oval, and a triangle in an indicated number of cells (i.e., squares of notebook paper).

To develop some understanding of spatial relations: up-down, in front-in back, to the left-to the right, adjacent-opposite; counting off a given number of cells from top to bottom and from left to right. To get the children to know printed and written numerals and to be able to distinguish between them (but not to be able to write them)

THIRD QUARTER

Formulation of Simple Problems. Familiarization with the structure of a problem: the condition, the numerical facts, the question involved, and the understanding of the relationships between the numerical facts of the problem; the formulation of problems based on the personal experiences of the children; the formulation of problems with varied content (with and without graphic materials). To develop the ability to formulate an arithmetical operation; to acquaint the children with the operational symbols: $+$ for addition, $-$ for subtraction, $=$ for equality. To formulate problems through a numerical example, using printed or written numerals. The solution of addition problems involving the addition of a smaller number to a greater one, and the solution of subtraction problems when the minuend (the number subtracted) is less than the difference: i.e., mastering techniques of adding on or taking away by units. To distinguish in a problem the operations of addition and subtraction and to give answers to problems, using specific numbers and symbols (saying them out). To name the digits in order and in reverse order, beginning with any particular digit; to be able to name the consecutive digits up to a given digit (which has either been named or indicated by the numeral), to name the digit which precedes and that which follows a given digit, and to understand the expressions "up to" and "after."

FOURTH QUARTER

Review of the material covered.

Drawing and Painting, Modeling, Cutting and Pasting, Construction

It is extremely important to give the child the desire to improve his drawing, painting, modeling, and cutting ability; to develop effective perceptiveness and visual memory; to excite the imagination and creativity of the child; to develop his appreciation of art (looking at pictures, sculpture, illustrations, designs); and to attract the child's attention to the richness of color and form in the surrounding world.

FIRST QUARTER

Drawing and Painting: The children learn to recognize the similarities and contrasts of objects in their form, structure, coloring, size, and characteristic features; and to convey such features in painting from nature and from memory. In their paintings the children reflect their impressions of the woods or a park in autumn, convey the colors of autumn, and the different shapes and colors of trees and bushes; they observe different means of transportation and the construction of a house, and portray what they have seen in their own way. They make symmetrical designs on strips, squares, and circles, using as the design elements leaves, flowers, and berries, or geometrical figures of various types—circles, arcs, and points. The designs are either drawn in pencil or painted. It is important for the children to be able to use, distinguish, and name the various colors of the spectrum (red, orange, yellow, green, blue, violet) and the neutral colors (black, white, dark gray, and light gray).

In illustrating the theme of a literary work, the children should be able to arrange the various elements properly in space, using a broad strip of ground, separated from the sky: further to the right, further to the left, higher up and lower (i.e., nearer and further away), but without observing the rules of perspective.

It is important to teach the children to handle a brush easily: to use the slanted position for making wide stripes and large spots and the vertical position when painting with the tip of the brush. The children develop the ability to spread the paint evenly on all parts of the picture; to outline things lightly in pencil; to paint with light, regular strokes; and to change the direction of the strokes to correspond to the shape of the object being represented.

Modeling: The children learn to model out of a single lump of clay not only objects with simple shapes (vegetables, fruits), but also ones with more complicated shapes (birds, horses, dolls) assembling the traditional ceramic toy figures. In making the latter, they rely on their accumulated knowledge of such forms as spheres, cylinders, ovals, cones, and discs. The children apply the various modeling techniques previously mastered and learn to paint and decorate their models with designs and then to use them in their play.

Cutting and Pasting: The children are taught to cut symmetrical forms out of paper, leaves and petals which have been folded in half. They continue to cut the parts for various shaped objects from paper of all different colors. They arrange the parts into attractive patterns and paste them onto a piece of paper (fall flowers, a branch with autumn leaves, a house with flags, a truck, a rug).

Construction: The children observe the different types of transportation and the buiding of a house, examine pictures and illustrations with these themes, and then convey their own impressions by constructing things from building materials. The children make things out of all different sorts of building materials, working from their own conception of a thing, a demonstration, a model, or a picture; they build toys from memory, from real life, or from a mock-up, receiving partial or full demonstrations of the techniques involved. The children learn to divide any quadrilateral figure along a diagonal, to divide a circle along a diameter, to cut along a straight line up to a given point by eye, to cut precisely along a straight or curved line; and to make curved lines.

SECOND QUARTER

Drawing and Painting: The children learn to paint various objects from real life; to convey their shape, structure, and characteristic coloring (a branch of a spruce or pine tree, fish, birds, toys, and dolls); to represent from memory objects and groups of objects related by a single theme (our playground, a New Year's Tree, trees in the snow, a street in the city); and to have the objects in the drawing conform to the size of the paper. In activity periods the children must be taught to select the type of paper which best fits the theme of the drawing they are planning. Themes for paintings and drawings may be literary works (poems and fairy tales such as "Lisichka-sestrichka and the Wolf," "The Geese and the Swans," "Morozko," and others).

The children make designs using colored backgrounds. They learn to make well-balanced designs on pieces of paper in the form of a rectangle or polygon, to combine large and small elements, and to introduce various flourishes into their designs. They are introduced to new colors (pink, light blue, bright yellow) and they learn to distinguish the bright and dark colors.

Modeling: [The children learn to] represent a moving figure in their model, to make two or three figures all based on a single theme, to paint and decorate their models with designs and to use them in their play.

Cutting and Pasting: [The children] cut out simple silhouette figures by eye from a piece of paper (birds, hares, etc.), and convey their characteristic shape; [they] cut out symmetrical designs and various objects from a piece of paper folded over twice.

Construction: The children build tall structures with roofs and embellishments, observing the correct proportions, symmetry, and balance; they learn how to set toys in motion using string. The children are taught to understand the significance of the various types of lines employed in patterns and models: hatch-marks indicating pieces which are to be pasted together, dotted lines indicating where to fold, and connected lines indicating where to cut. The children learn to make toys by following simple patterns.

THIRD QUARTER

Drawing and Painting: The children learn to convey the structure and the characteristic details of various things in nature (branches with buds on them, just before the leaves appear; the first spring flowers; shoots planted by the children themselves; seeds). From memory and on the basis of their observations, the children depict in their drawings groups of objects all related by a common theme (ice drifts, an orchard in blossom, a flight of birds, a factory, a mill). Utilizing the various skills they have acquired, the children are able to represent more fully and more colorfully their impressions of the First of May celebration, fairy tale episodes, and episodes from other literary works (poems about spring, about the Eighth of March, and about the First of May; the fairy tales "Ivan, the Tsarevich," "The Sick Bird," "The Golden Key"; the short stories "Four Wishes," "The Morning Rays" by Ushinsky, and others). Attractive paintings by the children are used to decorate the common rooms on holidays. The children paint motley bouquets, branches with blossoms on them, and berries using dark paper in the shape of a rectangle or oval.

Modeling: The children do collective work, learning to make their own figures conform in size to those of the other children ("Grandfather Mazai and the Hares," a chicken farm, a zoo, etc.).

Cutting and Pasting: The children continue to master the art of cutting out silhouette figures; they make silhouettes of characters in fairy tales to use in playing "magic lantern," ("Kolobok," "The Fox and the Hares," etc.); they paste on various figures to make landscapes, and fill up a large area with trees in blossom, ice breakers, etc.; they work collectively on large cutting and pasting projects (a meadow covered with flowers, cars riding along a highway, etc.).

Construction: The children make toys by themselves for the games they have devised, selecting the appropriately shaped pieces from ready-made paper figures, scraps of wood, and bits and pieces of material.

FOURTH QUARTER

In the summer the children apply the skills they have acquired and make use of the impressions they receive from nature and surrounding life. From real life they draw trees, field flowers, and berries; they model large figures of animals; and they make designs of flowers, berries, branches, beetles, butterflies, and birds. Collectively the children engage in large cutting and pasting projects (a bouquet of large flowers, fish in the water, branches laden with apples, etc.). The things made by the children are used in their play, in decorating the verandas, and in adorning the playground for holidays.

Physical Development

It is essential further to improve the children's running and walking ability: walking with a long stride with free and natural arm movements, running lightly and gracefully, walking and running at a fixed pace, and being able to change pace rapidly. The child's spatial orientation must be improved and his sense of balance further developed. The child's ability to jump from a standstill and to do running high jumps and broad jumps is developed, as is his accuracy in various throwing techniques; through instruction in climbing, the child's gracefulness and coordination are improved. It is very important to teach the children to find their own places again when running and walking; to form even columns, ranks, and circles; and to perform exercises precisely, gracefully, and at the indicated tempo. In exercises the children should develop greater coordination of their arm, leg, and body movements.

FIRST QUARTER

Walking, Running, Exercises for Balance: [The children] walk and run one behind the other, singly and in pairs, changing direction on a command from the teacher; walk and run in snakelike fashion, around a circle, not holding hands, and at changing speeds. [They] walk and run along a board or bench (width 15–20 centimeters, height 30–40 centimeters), along a log (horizontal and tilted), forward and sideways (diameter of the log 10–15 centimeters).

Jumping: Jumping up from a standstill [position] and with a running start, with the goal of reaching an object suspended 10–12 centimeters above the outstretched arms of the child. Jumping down from a height of 30–40 centimeters and landing smoothly.

Throwing: Throwing a ball up and catching it with two hands (eight or ten times in a row without dropping it); throwing a ball back and forth to each other from behind the head (distance 1½–2 meters).

Climbing: Getting from one span to another in climbing on a gymnastic apparatus.

SECOND QUARTER

Walking, Running, Exercises for Balance: [The children] walk and run off in all directions in a confined area of the hall or playground, giving way to each other and not bumping into one another, and stopping quickly at a signal; [they] walk on tiptoe and on their heels (1½–2 meters). [They] walk on all fours along a board, bench or log.

Jumping: Hopping from one foot to the other both in place and moving forward; doing standing broad jumps (50–70 centimeters).

Throwing: Throwing and catching a ball with one hand. Throwing and catching a ball while clapping hands. Throwing balls and snowballs at moving targets.

Climbing: Climbing between two poles, under a bench and through a hoop.

THIRD QUARTER

Walking, Running, Exercises for Balance: [The children are taught] to jump under a moving jump rope; to perform various simple actions while walking and running (avoiding touching objects, gathering up objects and moving them from place to place). To walk along a cord laid out in a straight line, around a circle, a zigzag, placing the heel of the front foot as close as possible to the toe of the rear foot; to walk along a board, bench, or log while performing additional tasks (stepping over objects, turning around, squatting, etc.).

Jumping: Doing a running broad jump (50–70 centimeters). Skipping rope individually and with a long rope held by two other children.

Throwing: Throwing balls and bags at horizontal and vertical targets— 3 meters with the right hand, and 2 meters with the left.

Climbing: Climbing on various gymnastic apparatuses, and climbing ladders and rope ladders (height 2–2½ meters).

FOURTH QUARTER

Walking, Running, Exercises for Balance: [The children] walk and run obstacle courses (climbing over and under things, stepping across things); run races and dodge away from the person chasing. [They] walk along the ground, on a board, or on a log while balancing something on the head.

Jumping: Doing running broad jumps (70–100 centimeters), running high jumps (30–40 centimeters).

Throwing: Tossing a ball back and forth over a net which is raised to a level slightly above the level of the children's heads (throwing with both hands). Throw balls for distance with either the left or right hand (not less than 4–5 meters).

Climbing: Scrambling on all fours up and down inclined boards and ladders.

Exercises for the Development of Specific Groups of Muscles

Exercises for the Shoulder Muscles   Raise the hands forward and up while simultaneously raising oneself up on tiptoe, heels together, tips of the feet apart, hands down (hands to the shoulders, hands behind the head). From a sitting or standing position, extend the arms to the side from behind the head while twisting the body alternately to the right and to the left. Touch the left shoulder with the right hand and the right shoulder with the left hand, extend the arms to the side, and then touch the shoulders again. With the arms bent at the elbows, energetically extend the forearms forward (fingers clenched into fists).
Stretch the elbows backwards two or three times in a row, and extend the arms to the side from a position right in front of the chest. Rotate the arms circularly, forward and backward, alternately and simultaneously. Pass a ball over the head from one to another, backward and forward.

Exercises for the Leg Muscles: Do knee bends while extending the arms forward and up, with and without objects. Do knee bends while holding onto one's back or the back of a table. Kick forward with the right leg while clapping the hands under the leg. While bending at the knees, alternately lift the right and left leg while transferring an object (cube, ball) from one hand to the other. Step backward and forward across a short rope, pole, or hoop held in the hands. While sitting on the floor grasp an object between the toes, bring the legs back in, and then extend them straight out; transfer an object from the toes of the right foot to the toes of the left foot. Walk sidewards along a pole, bringing the feet together at each step, and similarly walk forward, only alternating the right and left feet.

Exercises for the Muscles of the Torso Turn to the right and to the left while passing an object to the child standing next to or behind one. Bend forward with a pole across the shoulders or under the arms (legs straight, looking forward). Bend forward, place an object to the side of the right foot (left foot), and then take it up again. Bend to the side with a pole across the shoulders or with the hands placed on the waist (standing and sitting). While sitting with the arms extended backward, raise and lower the outstretched legs. While sitting on the floor lift both feet across a pole (rope). Sit with the legs crossed, bend forward to the right and the left knee, touching them with the forehead (using the arms to push the head down).

Drills and Formations

[The children are taught] to form quickly into single and double columns, circles, and ranks without assistance; to even up the columns, circles, and ranks; while in movement to shift from a single column into several, to shift from one circle into several circles; to make right and left turns.

Active Games

"Take It and Pass It on Quickly," "Change the Object," "Who Can Roll His Hoop to the Flag First," "Relay Race," "Blind Man's Buff," "Two Grandfathers Frost," "Dust Pan," "Who Can Get the Ribbon Off First," "The Heron and the Frog," "Bird Flight," "Monkey Catch," "Whoever is Called Catches the Ball," "The Hunters and the Beasts," "Relay Races with Balls," "Ball School," "Stop," etc.

Sports

Sleigh riding [The children are taught] to be able while sledding down a small hill to take up an object which has previously been placed on the slope, to push each other along, to slide down along icy paths from the top of a small icy slope.

Skiing [The children learn] to walk along a ski trail in a column. To walk cross-country (hills, slopes). To make right and left turns by crossing the skis over in place. To climb up and ski down hills by themselves (straight down and on a diagonal). To take off their skis by themselves. To carry their skis over their shoulders. To keep their skis in good order.

Skating [The children are taught] to assume the right starting position: legs bent slightly, body leaning forward, head held erect, and eyes looking straight forward. To spring up and down several times in this position. To stand and walk on skates along snow and on ice. To take a short run (three or four steps) and slide on both feet. To make right and left turns while sliding on both feet after a running start. Pushing off alternately with both feet, to slide on first the right and then the left foot. To put ice skates on by oneself.

Cycling [The children learn] to ride a bicycle without the assistance of an adult, and to make right and left turns. To ride around in a circle. To ride scooters (with the right and left foot).

Bathing (preparation for swimming) To play and splash around in a shallow stream, lake, or pool. To inhale and exhale in the water (three or four times in a row). To float on the stomach and on the back and to kick the legs up and down while walking along the bottom on the hands. To swim with an inflated toy or to swim around in a circle on the hands. If possible, to try to swim without support.

Musical Training

[*Objectives*]

To instill in the children a lasting interest in music, to foster a love for music, and to build up a repertory of familiar musical works

To expand conceptions of social and natural phenomena and to develop in the child an esthetic response to them

To strengthen the cultural pattern of listening to music and to intensify the child's emotional response to music; to develop the child's memory by having him try to recognize isolated parts of a composition; to teach the child to distinguish and correctly name dances, lullabies, and marches

To have the child form elementary concepts of the contents of a song or piece; of its form (introduction, conclusion, solo part, refrain, different voice parts); of the most striking means of conveying expression (fast-slow, loud-soft); and of the fact that music is written by composers (Glinka, Tchaikovsky, Krasev, Kabalevsky, etc).

To develop the child's ability to recognize pieces which are familiar to him and to encourage him to express his own feelings toward musical works.

Further objectives are: to teach the children to perform with expression songs, dances, and musical games, both individually and in groups, and to observe proper posture while singing and while moving in time to the music; to preserve the children's voices by electing songs with a limited range; to reinforce systematically acquired habits and skills by repeating the repertory learned in the previous groups; to develop in the children an ear for melody by stressing proper singing—maintaining correct pitch, making the correct intervals; to develop a sense of rhythm by requiring more subtle differentiation of movements corresponding to the character of the music, changes from one part to another, changes in the tempo, changes in the rhythm, etc.; to develop the ability of the children to portray independently characters in musical games and to apply familiar elementary dance steps in new combinations.

Singing The children [are taught] to sing with expression: to sing in a bright resonant voice, melodiously, and with a light tone. To take a breath before the beginning of a song and between musical phrases; to pronounce the words of a song distinctly, projecting the vowel sounds correctly and pronouncing final consonants. To perform at an indicated tempo, to accelerate, retard, make crescendos and diminuendos; to end musical phrases smoothly, to keep the rhythm precisely; to keep on tune; to listen to themselves and to others; and to perform familiar songs with and without accompaniment. The children should be able to distinguish high and low notes, long and short notes, and a rise or fall in the melody.

Musical Rhythmic Movements The children should be able to make their movements correspond to variations in the music; in the dynamics (crescendos, decrescendos) and in the pitch (higher and lower within an octave). They should be able to accelerate and decelerate their movements; to emphasize through their movements the beat, the time, and the simple rhythmic patterns; to alter their movements to correspond with musical phrases; to begin their movements independently after the musical introduction is completed.

The children should be taught to perform the following movements to music: to walk triumphantly, softly, and smoothly; to run lightly and gracefully; to lope; to hop from one foot to the other, varying the movement with the music (lightly and heavily); to execute various moves smoothly and energetically, with and without objects. They should become better oriented in space; they should be able to walk in ranks while performing folk and circle dances, to portray various characters with expression, conveying their most characteristic features (a cowardly hare, a sly fox, etc.). To perform dance steps: a polka step, an alternating step, a tap step, a squat, a leap sideways, etc.; to perform dances consisting of these steps expressively and to utilize these steps in improvising their own dances. The children should know the terms for the most basic dance steps.

FIRST QUARTER

Music for Listening: "Harvest," music by M. Krasev; "Children's Polka," music by M. Glinka; "Lullaby," music by N. Rimsky-Korsakov; "October Song," music by M. Krasev; "Waltz," music by N. Levy.

Singing: "Treacle and Ginger," "A Fox Was Walking in the Woods," Russian folk lullabies; "The Leaves are Falling," music by M. Krasev; "October Holiday," music by Y. Slonov; "The Geese," music by A. Filippenko; "Sleep, Yanichek," Czech folk song.

Games to Songs and Instrumental Music: "The Snowball Tree," "The Hare," "The Fence," Russian folk songs; "Take the Flag," Hungarian folk tune; "Welcome, Autumn," music by V. Vitlin; "A Trip to the City," music by V. Gerchik.

Dances and Exercises: "Polka," music by M. Glinka; "The Windmill," "Swinging Arms," music by T. Lomova; "Pair Dance," Karelian folk tune; "The Races," music by B. Mozhevelov.

SECOND QUARTER

Music for Listening: "Why the Bear Sleeps in Winter," music by L. Knipper; "The Doll's Sickness," "The New Doll," music by P. Tchaikovsky; "Cavalry Song," music by D. Kabalevsky; "Lullaby," music by V. Vitlin.

Singing: "Winter Song," music by M. Krasev; "It's Nice in Our Garden," music by V. Gerchik; "Our Song Is Simple," music by A. Alexandrov; "The Fir Tree," music by L. Beckman; "We Are Friendly Kids," music by S. Razorenov.

Games to Songs and Instrumental Music: "Thin Ice," Russian folk song; "The Fox and the Hares," music by M. Krasev; "What Kind of Tree is This?" music by M. Starokadomsky, "The Beasts and the Hunter," music by E. Tilicheeva; "Search," music by T. Lomova.

Dances and Exercises: "Dance of the Snowflakes," music by A. Zhilina; "The Fleecy Clouds," Russian folk song; "The Puppets," music by A. Dargomyzhsky; "The New Year," Polish folk song.

THIRD QUARTER

Music for Listening: "Grandchildren of Lenin," music by V. Vitlin; "The Bird House," music by D. Kabalevsky; "Song of the Wood Larks," music by P. Tchaikovsky; "Dance of the Birds," music by N. Rimsky-Korsakov; "Kamarinskaya" (a lively Russian folk dance), music by P. Tchaikovsky; "The Gay Peasant," music by R. Schumann.

Singing: "May Holiday," "Flag of the First of May," music by M. Krasev; "Portrait of Ilyich," music by L. Schul'gin; "A Birch Tree Stood in the Field," Russian folk song; "On the Bridge," music by A. Filippenko; "Petya, the Drummer," music by M. Krasev; "Our Mother," music by Y. Slonov.

Games to Songs and Instrumental Music: "Chernozen—the Black Earth," Russian folk song; "Let's Build a House," music by E. Tilicheeva; "Kolobok," Russian folk song; "Who's the Fastest?" music by L. Shwartz; "The Saplings," music by E. Tilicheeva; "Colored Flags," Estonian folk dance; "Carousel," Russian folk tune.

Dances and Exercises: "Russian Dance," Russian folk tune; "The Ball," "The Jump Rope," music by I. Petrov; "Change Couples," Ukranian folk tune; "Annusha," Czech polka; "Flag Exercise," Russian folk tune. "Poidu L'Ya, Vyidu L'Ya," circle dance (Russian folk tune).

FOURTH QUARTER

Music for Listening: "We're Flying Away to the Moon," music by V. Vitlin; "Turkish March," music by W. Mozart.

Singing: "We're Going to School," music by Y. Slonov; "Summer Flowers," music by E. Tilicheeva; "Farewell to Thee, Our Kindergarten," Hungarian folk song adapted by T. Popatenko; "The Apple," music by E. Tilicheeva.

Games to Songs and Instrumental Music: "We Shall Go to the Green Meadows," music by N. Levy; "The Castle," "The Round Loaf," "Playing Catch," Russian folk songs; "Exercising," music by M. Starakadomsky; "The Garland," Hungarian folk song.

Dances and Exercises

"The Ball Exercise," music by T. Lomova.

PLAY

In the older group play serves to deepen the child's interest in the events taking place in our country, in construction, and in technology, to develop social feelings and to strengthen the feeling of collectivism. It also serves to develop the child's imagination and initiative and to satisfy the child's need for activity. While playing, the children join together, communicate with each other, agree on a theme for their games, share roles, and follow a definite order in the actions involved in the game. The quality of perseverance in fulfilling what they have set out to do is observable in children of this age. A stable collective is created through play.

The sphere of conceptions formed as a result of the assimilation of the material in the program, the personal contact with people, and the reading of artistic literature is reflected in the breadth of interests evidenced by the child's play and the creative ideas he introduces into his games. The structures he builds are distinguished by their great variety, impressive size, correctness in the disposition of the parts, stability, and diversity of decorations.

In group dramatization games, the children's artistic capabilities and their ability to organize themselves develop. An important role is played by active games involving rules, sports, and entertaining activities in which the children have their best opportunity to reveal their potentiality for self-organization. In active games such physical attributes as speed, agility, and accuracy are developed, as is the ability to submit to the rules of a game and to see that they are observed. The children also enjoy active games in which there is an element of competition—team games. Educational games that involve mental efforts and keenness and that satisfy the cognitive interests of the children are introduced into their daily routine. Games become longer in duration.

Morning Play

The morning play activities of the children evolve easily and naturally since many of them arrive in the kindergarten with their interests and intentions already determined; or they simply continue games begun on the previous day, fixing up or adding to structures they were building, etc.

The teacher's objective during this morning period is to stimulate the children's desires to join in interesting group games. The teacher strives to penetrate the children's thoughts and plans and, wherever necessary, she helps them to decide on a game and to agree among themselves.

Various role-playing and building games as well as ball games are very useful in organizing the children into groups.

Play between Activity Periods

Play at these times gives the children a chance to satisfy their need for physical activity. Particularly suitable are games involving running, throwing and catching ("Catch the Ball," "Bilboquet," "Who's Faster?" "Who's Agile?"), and active games involving rules ("Find Your Partner," "Bear Cubs"). In selecting and organizing these games, the teacher must take into consideration the nature of the activities just concluded; thus after physical exercises and musical activities, the children can continue the games begun in the morning; whereas after an activity in which the children were seated at tables, it is advisable to involve them in very active games such as playing ball and games involving running. At the very end of this recreational break, the teacher and the children on duty remind the other children that it is time to end their play and begin the activities.

Outdoor Play

The morning outdoor play period may extend for over two hours. The teacher's objective during this period is to organize games that will contibute to the physical development of the children and that will unite them in a friendly atmosphere. The children should know what equipment and materials are brought out for the outdoor recreation period; they are trained to carry these out and to make sure that after they have finished playing, they are returned to their places.

At the beginning of the outdoor play period, the teacher should encourage games involving running, throwing, walking along logs and climbing, since these will give the children a chance to relax and "let off steam" after the activities. Active games with rules ("The Sly Fox," "Wolf in a Rage") and various types of catching, running, and jumping games should be organized when the children have already been playing independently for some time. Then the children will form into groups voluntarily and may play any of a great variety of games: building and role-playing games, sports, etc. In the fall, with observations and artistic literature serving as stimuli, the children actively engage in thematic role-playing games such as playing "Pioneers," "Travel," and "*Kolkhoz.*"

When the children are outside in the winter it is preferable to have them play games that will enable them to warm up quickly: games involving running, jumping, and throwing, such as "Snow Circles," "Two Grandfathers Frost," "Knock the Cap off the Snow Woman," etc. The children get practice in running and in throwing snowballs at targets and for distance. Active games make the outdoor play periods enjoyable for the children regardless of the weather and are a valuable means of strengthening and conditioning the children's bodies.

It is advisable to organize such sports as skiing and ice skating at the beginning of the outdoor play period, immediately after activities. The teacher helps the children to handle the sports equipment in the proper fashion.

In winter the children enjoy building things out of snow and decorating them with blocks of ice and colored flags, as well as devising role-playing games with various different themes. The children will occasionally build structures out of snow which are related to the subjects of literary works (ships, trains, the types of huts lived in by the nationalities of the north, etc.). In such play, an interest is developed in the lives and feats of the people of other nationalities; the desire to design, construct, and equip is stimulated.

In the spring and summer especially, the children enjoy games involving jumping, climbing, and running.

Before the children go outdoors for recreation, it is helpful to talk with them about what they intend to play and what they will need to bring out with them. The outdoor play period begins with the children playing individually with toys and at various types of individual sports. Jump ropes, hoops, balls, and bicycles are widely used. After these individual games, the teacher should suggest more relaxed play, such as playing with sand and water and playing such games as, for example, "Storm at Sea," "Telephone Out of Order," "Guess Whose Voice," "What Is the Object in the Riddle?" etc. The children in this group should know very well the rules of conduct involved in play, what is allowed and what is forbidden. In a sheltered area or under trees, the children engage in role-playing games, dramatization games, circle games, and games involving singing: "The Castle," "At Our Gates," "The Raven." To play with in the woods, fields, or on the bank of a stream the children take shovels, pails, balls, and jump ropes. The children independently organize their favorite active games—"Rescue," "Geese and Swans," etc. The teacher explains new games.

It is important to get the children to play games involving throwing at targets and throwing for distance and jumping up and stretching out their arms ("Reach the Rope," etc.). Such games require the supervision of the teacher. In order to improve the children's sense of balance, the teacher encourages such physical activities as walking along a board, a log, or a rope and walking with a bag balanced on the head ("Don't Drop the Bag"). The children who have trouble following the rules of a game are put into groups with others who have already mastered the rules.

The children play role-playing and building games on the playground. The children are interested in the work involved in caring for animals and satisfy this interest in a variety of games: "Cow Pasture," Chicken Farm," "Horse Farm," and "Zoo." For making their structures the children use crates, plywood, boards, fir cones, branches, stones, and sand. The teacher shows the children sensible building techniques, demonstrates how to make floors and ceilings, and shows the children different ways to decorate their buildings.

There should be an area on the playground with a large mound of sand that can be used for large building projects (a city, a *kolkhoz,* a park, a pioneer camp). The children enjoy using sand, clay, and water in their constructions, as it enables them to make the projects more intricate and to devise role-playing games to go along with them; it also stimulates them to build toys out of wood or other natural materials for use in these games. A comfortable spot should be set aside for this type of handicraft.

Through different variants of the game "*Kolkhoz,*" the teacher arouses the curiosity and interest of children who live in the city in the work performed on the *kolkhozes*—plowing, sowing, reaping, milling flour, and raising domestic animals. Toy sets with plows, seeders, and tractors (the teacher explains the functions of the various machines and equipment), as well as the sets called "Chicken Farm" and "Cattle Farm," help in the organization of meaningful group games.

As a result of looking at pictures and slides and actively participating in role-playing and building games (playing "Pilots," "Airplanes," "Ships," "Sailors," "Railroad," etc.) the children's interest in the work of aviators, railroad workers, etc. is deepened.

In playing "Railroad," for example, the children learn in the process of their activity that grain and vegetables are shipped to the cities while goods manufactured in the cities for the *kolkhoz* workers are delivered to the village stores.

Games involving trains and traveling to see the Nentsi, Uzbeks, Tadzhiks, and other peoples broaden the child's outlook and arouses his interest in the way of life of people of other nationalities.

Play Following the Afternoon Nap

During this play period, the teachers strive to develop the individual interests of the children and to promote independence, creative activity, and the ability of the children to play and work together. The children play in small groups, joining with their particular friends or with those who share with them a common interest. The teacher encourages and works to develop those games that will foster a collective spirit; will further the children's interest in work; and will help to develop creativity, imagination, initiative, and cleverness.

The children join together in construction games through common interests and the urge to learn to build large, solid, and attractive houses, just like the ones in their street; buildings similar to the best ones in their city; kindergartens; schools; and buildings like the great ones in Moscow that they have seen in pictures.

In the evening it is good for the teacher to talk over with the children the games they are planning as well as the ones they have just completed and possible subjects for future construction; in this way, she discovers the individual and collective interests of the group.

The teacher encourages independent preparation by the children for dramatization games: "Repka," "The Castle," and "The Wolf and the Seven Little Goats." The children by themselves model toys to be used in shows, prepare decorations, and start musical games on their own, benefiting from their experiences in musical activity periods. The teacher can suggest that they listen to music and songs on records, sing their favorite songs, listen to stories, look at pictures in a book, or watch slides.

In many of the games played outdoors during the time allotted for independent activity, the children may, on their own initiative, sing; listen to records; pick out very simple tunes on the toy xylophones; and play educational musical games, which develop their ear for music, their sense of rhythm, and their memory for music. Music becomes a part of the daily life of the children. They enjoy introducing the singing of familiar songs into their games. They sing traditional Russian songs such as "Skok-poskok"; "Andrei the Sparrow"; "In the Park or in the Garden"; "The Calf"; and "We Are Friendly Kids," S. Razorenov; and "The Apple," E. Tilicheeva.

For marches, the following songs are used: "We Are Happy Kids," M. Raukhverger; "Petya, the Drummer," "March," M. Krasev; "Morning Exercise," M. Starokadomsky.

Also available on records are the following marching songs: "Parade," E. Tilicheeva; "The Gay Team," M. Blanter; "Pioneers' March," G. Gabichvadze; "Halt, Who Goes?" B. Solov'ev-Sedoi.

The following works are recommended for dancing: "Doll's Polka," A. Zhivtsov; "Waltz," S. Maikapar; "Let's Go to the Raspberry Garden," A. Filippenko, Russian folk dances.

The teacher may let the children listen to any record of their choice.

For individual play on xylophones, the following Russian folk songs are particularly appropriate: "The Sun," "On the Green Meadow," "Under the Arch by the City," and "The Cow," music by M. Raukhverger.

Types of Games

Role-playing Games Various types of creative games reflecting the work of adults grow out of a desire on the part of the children to imitate adults and be like adults in their conduct and actions. Games such as "Factory," "Mill," "Construction," "*Kolkhoz*," "Freight Train," "School," "Family," "Library," etc., give the teacher an opportunity to train the children to apply in their play the things they have learned in the activity periods; to broaden the interest of the children in workers, the machines they operate, and the products of their labor; to develop a feeling of enjoyment in work; and to develop cognitive and artistic abilities. In games related to routine living, work habits are reinforced and the children develop a desire to introduce beauty and comfort into daily life. The teacher expands the interests of the children and develops their imagination through the subject matter of the particular game. She broadens their ideas about the type of activity involved in various occupations and the interrelationships between them: the pilot and the radio man on an airplane; the captain, the helmsman, and the sailor on a ship.

Games with Building Materials These games are useful and necessary for the creative development of the child. In these games he is trained to assemble objects and buildings; he learns the relationships between the parts, how to arrange the parts, and how to decorate the structures.

In construction games the teacher further develops in the child spatial concepts and concepts of the form, size, quantity and quality of materials.

The children build things using the building materials of Mogilevsky "Architect." They attain in their structures close resemblances to drawings and designs: stations, apartment buildings, bridges, clubs, subway stations, pavilions, exhibits, cattle farms, houses, farms. The children become familiar with a completely new ceramic construction set consisting of many very small pieces of all different types. When they have learned how to put the pieces together, they attempt to make precise copies of the models provided and thus display their capacities, their perseverance, cleverness, and patience.

In working with the "Constructor" set of Polikarpov, the children learn more complicated methods of joining the pieces together and build larger structures. They examine an album of sketches and designs and attempt to build cranes, power shovels, etc.

In the second half of the year, the children are given the "Constructor-Mechanic No. 1" (designed by Sakharov). The children learn a new technique for joining pieces together with the help of a wrench and screw driver, a method requiring greater precision and greater manual dexterity. The children construct carts, chairs, wagons, cranes, suspension bridges, and automobiles and make simple vehicles out of blocks and wheels. This type of work requires the extremely attentive supervision of the teacher.

The children develop greater skill in building from designs, sketches, and photographs; from memory; and from the teacher's instructions. It is important to teach the children to try to visualize the thing they are trying to build. When the children run into difficulties, the teacher helps them to select the right pieces and teaches them how to fasten them together in different combinations. An effective technique is to show a model, challenge the child to guess how it was made, and then suggest that he try to make it.

Various types of natural materials are utilized on construction play: sand, clay, snow, fir cones, acorns, birch bark, branches, corncobs, etc.

Dramatization Games   These games help to develop expressiveness in the child's speech and movements, contribute to uniting the children, and lead to the accumulation of common artistic experiences and the development of creative potentialities. The children can dramatize on their own the poems of S. Marshak; "The Gloves"; the Russian fairy tale, "The Wolf and the Fox"; the fairy tale by the Brothers Grimm, "The Fox and the Geese"; etc.

Musical Games   The children enjoy musical games in that they combine interesting play elements with singing, rhythmic movements, and dances. In circle games, large groups of children join in together. The teacher introduces the new circle games; then when the children have learned them, they play these games by themselves ("We Shall Go into the Green Meadows," "The Castle," "Playing Catch").

Active Games   Active games satisfy the children's need to play together; to compete in speed, agility, and accuracy; and to attain the best result. The children themselves organize these games. They determine who will be the leader and who will play each role in the game, and then they watch carefully to see that everybody follows the rules. In this group, it is important to introduce widely games that will contribute to the development of agility, accuracy, coordination, and grace (hoop games, quoits, hopscotch, skip rope, catch, tossing a ball back and forth over a net, "Knock the Cap Off," "Who's Agile?"); games which include an element of competition between two children or two teams of children ("Catch Your Partner," "Spread the Pebbles Out," "Who Will Get to the Top First"). Rules are introduced requiring self-control on the part of the children ("Find and Then Keep Mum," "The Sly Fox," "Catch").

Each child should be able to organize an active game and serve as the leader.

The teacher shifts the children from one game to another and watches the behavior of the children during the games, preventing excessive excitement and encouraging friendliness and cooperation. The teacher explains new games, arousing the interest of the children in the point of the game, clarifying the rules, demonstrating any difficult positions involved in the game (skittles, hoopla, etc.).

Educational Games The children enjoy the opportunities afforded by educational games for demonstrating their knowledge, agility, shrewdness, and attention and for competing with the other children. They continue to enjoy the game elements involved, but they are now already more interested in the final goal and the necessity of making a real effort to attain the desired success. For the school preparatory group there should be games that will develop general abilities, initiative, organizational skill, judgment, and self-control (various types of mosaics, games based on the classification of objects, the lotto games "To Each What He Needs" and "The Seasons," etc.).

Games including elements of physical and mental competition are somewhat more complicated: tenpins, checkers, tiddlywinks, spillikins, "Who's Agile?" "Table Croquet," etc. Games in which the children have a chance to utilize the knowledge and skills they have acquired are particularly useful: dominoes; arithmetic lotto; "Learning to Count"; "ABC"; the lotto game "From Sound to Letter"; puzzle games, and verbal games such as "Storm at Sea," "Black and White," "What's the Object in the Riddle?" etc.

The teacher encourages the children's desires to play various educational games, taking into consideration meanwhile individual differences in their stages of development; in certain cases she will advise a child to play the specific games that will prove most useful for him. The teacher shows her approval whenever she notices in the children's play good organization, good friendly relations among the children, and the application of a clever counting-out method for organizing a game.

Musical Educational Games   Guess the instrument (xylophone, rattle, tambourine, cymbals); repeat the sound (using two xylophones); musical echo, figure out the song suggested by the picture and sing it (musical lotto); play your favorite song on the phonograph (toy phonograph).

HOLIDAYS AND CELEBRATIONS

Holidays are big events in the lives of the children, giving them vivid and happy experiences. Six-year-old children perceive the Soviet holidays not merely as kindergarten holidays but also as joyful events in the life of society.

Triumphantly celebrated in the kindergarten are the holidays of the October Revolution, the First of May, and the Eighth of March. The teacher organizes excursions through the streets, where the children observe the busy holiday preparations. The children decorate the portrait of V. I. Lenin with flowers.

The children participate actively in preparing for and celebrating the New Year's holiday.

Along with the rehearsed performances (choruses, dances, dramatizations, and poetry readings), it is wise to include in the program for the morning parties things which have not been prepared such as lively games, dances, jokes, surprise gifts, and performances by adults (choruses, etc.).

The child's entrance into school is an important event in his life. A morning party marking this event is organized at the end of August. At the party the children sing, dance, recite poems, and perform gymnastics.

For the morning parties, the children clean the common rooms and playground thoroughly, prepare presents for the younger children and for their parents, and prepare invitations for guests.

In preparing for parties, one must not overburden the children or disrupt the daily schedule.

Holiday preparations contribute to developing the creative talents of the children.

In the older group, the children's birthdays are observed: gifts are made, a holiday table is laid, and individual musical performances are arranged.

Entertainment of the following types brings variety and happiness into the lives of the children: demonstrations of slides and films; puppet shows and "magic lantern" shows; adult performances (choruses and dances); and talent shows with dramatizations of fairy tales, poetry readings, riddles, jokes, and entertaining games.

Appendix

MODEL DAILY SCHEDULES FOR
THE DIFFERENT AGE GROUPS

Daily Schedule for Children in the First Infant Group

(from 3 months to 1 year)

	FROM 3 MOS. TO 5–6 MOS.	FROM 5–6 MOS. TO 9–10 MOS.	FROM 9–10 MOS. TO 1 YEAR
AT HOME			
Rising, feeding, waking period	6:00–7:00 A.M.	6:00–7:00 A.M.	
Rising, waking period			6:30–7:00 A.M.
IN THE KINDERGARTEN			
Receiving the children, inspection, changing clothes, play in the playpen (and on the floor)	7:00–8:00	7:00–8:00	7:00–8:00
Putting the children to bed, sleep in the fresh air	7:30–9:30	8:00–10:00	
Breakfast			7:30–8:30
Play, activities			8:30–9:00
Putting the children to bed, sleep in the fresh air			9:00–11:30
Gradual rising, feeding	9:30–10:00	10:00–10:45	
Gradual rising, dinner			11:30–12:30 P.M.
Waking period, play; activities	10:00–11:00	10:45–12:00 P.M.	12:30–2:30
Putting the children to bed, sleep in the fresh air	11:00–1:00 P.M.	12:00–2:00	2:30–4:00 P.M.
Gradual rising, feeding	1:00–1:30	2:00–2:45	
Gradual rising, afternoon snack			4:00–5:00
Waking period, play, activities	1:30–2:30	2:45–4:00	5:00–6:00
Putting children to bed, sleep in the fresh air	2:30–4:30	4:00–6:00	
Gradual rising, feeding	4:30–5:30	6:00–6:30	
Parents take children home	5:00	6:00	6:00
AT HOME			
Sleep	6:00–7:30		
Bathing, feeding	7:30–8:30		
Bathing, putting children to bed for the night		7:30–8:00	
Play, outdoor recreation			6:00–7:00
Bathing, supper			7:00–7:30
Night sleep	8:30–6:00 A.M.	8:00–6:00 A.M.	8:00–6:30 A.M.
Feeding	11:30 P.M.	10:00 P.M.	11:00 P.M.

Daily Schedule for Children in the Second Infant Group

(from 1 to 2 years—day attendance)

	FROM 1 TO 1½ YEARS	FROM 1½ TO 2 YEARS
AT HOME		
Rising, morning toilet	6:30–7:30 A.M.	6:30–7:30 A.M.
IN THE KINDERGARTEN		
Receiving the children, inspection, play	7:00–8:00	7:00–8:00
Preparation for breakfast, breakfast	7:30–8:30	7:45–8:30
Play	8:30–8:45	8:30–9:05
Activities	8:45–9:05	9:05–9:25
Play	9:05–9:20	
Preparation for sleep, sleep in the fresh air	9:20–11:45	
Play		9:25–9:40
Preparation for outside recreation, recreation and outside activities		9:40–11:00
Return from outside recreation, undressing		11:00–11:30
Gradual rising in the order in which the children awake, airbaths and water procedures	11:45–12:30 P.M.	
Preparation for dinner, dinner		11:30–12:00 P.M.
Preparation for sleep, sleep in the fresh air		12:00–3:00
Play and activities	12:30–3:00	
First activity	12:45–1:00	
Second activity	2:00–2:15	
Preparation for sleep, sleep in the fresh air	3:00–4:30	
Gradual rising in the order in which the children awake, airbaths and water procedures for the older subgroup, afternoon snack	4:30–5:30	3:00–4:30
Play, parents take children home, evening outside activity with parents	5:30–7:00	4:30–7:00
AT HOME		
Preparation for supper, supper (before supper—hygienic bath)	7:00–7:20	7:00–7:20
Play, evening toilet	7:20–8:00	7:20–8:00
Putting children to bed and night sleep	8:00–6:30 A.M.	8:00–6:30 A.M.

Daily Schedule for Children in the Second Infant Group

(from 1 to 2 years—24-hour attendance)

	FROM 1 TO 1½ YRS	FROM 1½ TO 2 YRS
Rising in the order in which the children awake, and water procedures, morning toilet, inspection, air-baths, play	7:00–8:00 A.M.	7:00–8:00 A.M.
Preparation for breakfast, breakfast	7:45–8:30	7:45–8:30
Play	8:30–8:45	8:30–9:05
Activities	8:45–9:05	9:05–9:25
Play	9:05–9:45	
Preparation for outdoor recreation, recreation and outdoor activities		9:25–11:00
Preparation for sleep, sleep in the fresh air	9:45–12:00	
Return from outdoor recreation, undressing		11:00–11:30
Preparation for dinner, dinner (younger children eat in shifts in the order in which they awake)	12:00–12:30 P.M.	11:30–12:00 P.M.
Preparation for sleep, sleep in the fresh air		12:00–3:00
Play and activities	12:30–3:30	
First activity	12:45–1:00	
Second activity	2:00–2:15	
Gradual rising after sleep		3:00–3:30
Play	2:15–3:00	
Preparation for afternoon snack, afternoon snack	3:30–4:00	3:30–3:50
Preparation for sleep, sleep in the fresh air	4:00–5:30	
Play		3:50–4:00
Activities		4:00–4:15
Preparation for outdoor recreation, recreation and outdoor activities		4:15–5:30
Return from outdoor recreation		5:30–6:00
Rising after sleep in the order in which the children awake	5:30–6:00	
Taking the children's temperature, play, activity	6:00–7:10	6:00–7:15
Preparation for supper, supper	7:10–7:40	7:15–7:35
Play	7:40–8:30	7:35–8:15
Preparation for sleep, before sleep—hygienic bath according to schedule	8:30–9:00	8:15–8:30
Night sleep	9:00–7:00 A.M.	8:30–7:00 A.M.

177

Comments In the spring-summer period the daily schedule for the children in the second infant group and all older groups changes. The length of the night sleep is shortened at the expense of a later bedtime and earlier rising (within a range of 40–60 minutes), the length of the day sleep is lengthened slightly, and dinner begins 30 minutes earlier.

The time spent by the children in the air is increased by having them spend every possible moment of the schedule in the playground, by shortening the time spent on the dressing and undressing of the children for outdoor recreation, and, in the older groups, at the expense of shortening one of the activities. Air and sun baths are taken more frequently (typically one hour before dinner.)

Daily Schedule for Children in the First Younger Group

(from 2 to 3 years—day attendance)

FALL-WINTER PERIOD

AT HOME

Rising, morning toilet	6:30–7:30 A.M.

IN THE KINDERGARTEN

Receiving the children, inspection, play	7:00–8:00
Preparation for breakfast, breakfast	7:50–8:35
Play—activities (in subgroups)	8:35–9:15–9:30
Preparation for outdoor recreation, recreation for children of first subgroup	9:15–11:15
Preparation for outdoor recreation, recreation for children of second subgroup	9:30–11:30
Gradual (in subgroups) return from outdoor recreation, undressing, play	11:15–11:30–11:40
Preparation for dinner, dinner	11:40–12:30 P.M.
Preparation for sleep, sleep in the fresh air	12:30–3:00–3:30
Rising after sleep in the order in which the children awake, air baths and water procedures, play	3:00–3:30–4:00
Preparation for afternoon snack, snack	4:00–4:30
Play, activities (in subgroups)	4:30–5:00
Play, children leave for home	5:00–7:00

AT HOME

Play	up to 7:20
Preparation for supper	7:20–8:15
Preparation for sleep	8:15–8:30
Night sleep	8:30–6:30–7:00 A.M.

178

Daily Schedule for Children in the First Younger Group

(from 2 to 3 years—24 hour attendance)

Rising in the order in which the children awake, morning toilet, air baths and water procedures, play	6:30–7:00–8:00 A.M.
Preparation for breakfast	7:50–8:35
Play, activities (in subgroups)	8:35–9:15–9:30
Preparation for outdoor recreation, recreation for children in first subgroup	9:15–11:15
Preparation for outdoor recreation, recreation for children in second subgroup	9:30–11:30
Gradual (by subgroups) return from outdoor recreation, undressing, play	11:15–11:30–11:40
Preparation for dinner, dinner	11:40–12:30 P.M.
Preparation for sleep, sleep in the fresh air	12:30–3:00–3:30
Rising in the order in which the children awake, air baths and water procedures, play	3:00–3:30–4:00
Preparation for afternoon snack, snack	4:00–4:30
Play, activities (in subgroups)	4:30–5:00–5:15
Preparation for outdoor recreation, recreation for children in first subgroup	5:00–6:25
Preparation for outdoor recreation, recreation for children in second subgroup	5:00–6:40
Gradual (by subgroups) return from outdoor recreation, undressing, play	6:25–7:20
Preparation for supper, supper	7:20–8:00
Play, evening toilet, preparation for sleep	8:00–8:30
Night sleep	8:30–6:30–7:00 A.M.

Daily Schedule for Children in the Second Younger Group

(from 3 to 4 years)

AT HOME

Rising, morning toilet	6:30–7:30

IN THE KINDERGARTEN

Receiving the children, inspection, play	7:00–8:00
Preparation for breakfast, breakfast	8:00–8:45
Play, preparation for activities	8:45–9:15
Activities	9:15–9:30
Preparation for outdoor recreation, recreation	9:30–12:00 P.M.

IN THE KINDERGARTEN

Preparation for dinner, dinner	12:00–12:45
Preparation for sleep, sleep	12:45–3:00
Rising from sleep, airbaths and water procedures, play	3:00–4:00
Preparation for afternoon snack, snack	4:00–4:30
Preparation for outdoor recreation, recreation. Children leave for home.	4:30–7:00

AT HOME

Play	7:00–7:30
Preparation for supper, supper	7:30–8:00
Relaxed play, preparation for sleep	8:00–8:30
Night sleep	8:30–6:30–7:00 A.M.

Comments Beginning with January or February, morning exercises are introduced into the schedule and performed regularly.

In the 24-hour groups, conditioning procedures are carried out in the morning after sleep.

Depending on local conditions at the kindergarten, the schedule can be somewhat altered with specific things moved up or back in the schedule, but not by more than a half-hour in either direction.

In the summer there is one activity: Musical training, observation of nature and people at work, reading and story-telling.

Daily Schedule for Children in the Middle Groups

(from 4 to 5 years)

FALL-WINTER PERIOD

AT HOME

Rising, morning toilet	6:30–7:30 A.M.

IN THE KINDERGARTEN

Receiving the children, inspection, play, work assignments, morning exercises	7:00–8:20
Preparation for breakfast, breakfast	8:20–9:00
Play, preparation for activities	9:00–9:30
Activities	9:30–9:50
Preparation for outdoor recreation, recreation	9:50–12:15 P.M.
Preparation for dinner, dinner	12:15–1:00
Preparation for sleep, sleep	1:00–3:00
Rising, airbaths and water procedures, play	3:00–3:50
Preparation for afternoon snack, snack	3:50–4:15
Play, preparation for outdoor recreation, recreation. Children leave for home.	4:15–7:00

AT HOME

Play	7:00–7:30
Preparation for supper, supper	7:30–7:50
Relaxed play, preparation for sleep	7:50–8:45
Night sleep	8:45–6:30–7:00 A.M.

180

Daily Schedule for Children in the Older Group

(from 5 to 6 years)

AT HOME

Rising, morning toilet	6:30–7:30 A.M.

IN THE KINDERGARTEN

Receiving the children, inspection, play-work assign- ments, morning exercises	7:00–8:30
Preparation for breakfast, breakfast	8:30–9:00
Play, preparation for activities	9:00–9:20
First activity	9:20–9:50
Second activity	10:00–10:20
Preparation for outdoor recreation, recreation	10:20–12:30 P.M.
Preparation for dinner, dinner	12:30–1:15
Preparation for sleep, sleep	1:15–3:00
Rising, airbaths and water procedures, play	3:00–4:00
Preparation for afternoon snack, snack	4:00–4:20
Preparation for outdoor recreation, recreation. Children leave for home.	4:20–7:00

AT HOME

Play	7:00–7:30
Preparation for supper, supper	7:30–7:50
Relaxed play, preparation for sleep	7:50–8:45
Night sleep	8:45–6:30–7:00 A.M.

Daily Schedule for School-Preparatory Group

(from 6 to 7 years)

AT HOME

Rising, morning toilet	6:30–7:30 A.M.

IN THE KINDERGARTEN

Receiving the children, inspection, work assignments, play and morning exercises	7:00–8:30
Preparation for breakfast, breakfast	8:30–9:00
Play, preparation for activities	9:00–9:20
First activity	9:20–9:50
Second activity	10:00–10:25

IN THE KINDERGARTEN

Preparation for outdoor recreation, recreation	10:25–12:30 P.M.
Preparation for dinner, dinner	12:30–1:15
Preparation for sleep, sleep	1:15–3:00
Rising, air baths and water procedures, play and work	3:00–4:15
Preparation for afternoon snack, snack	4:15–4:30
Preparation for outdoor recreation, recreation. Children leave for home.	4:30–7:00

AT HOME

Play	7:00–7:45
Preparation for supper, supper	7:45–8:10
Relaxed play, preparation for sleep	8:10–9:00
Night sleep	9:00–6:30–7:30 A.M.